Service Oriented Architecture with Java

Using SOA and web services to build powerful
Java applications

Binildas CA

Malhar Barai

Vincenzo Caselli

BIRMINGHAM - MUMBAI

Service Oriented Architecture with Java

First published: June 2008

Production Reference: 1180608

Published by Packt Publishing Ltd.
32 Lincoln Road
Olton
Birmingham, B27 6PA, UK.

ISBN 978-1-847193-21-6

www.packtpub.com

Cover Image by Nik Lawrence (Nik.Lawrence@Jaama.co.uk)

Credits

Authors

Binildas CA

Malhar Barai

Vincenzo Caselli

Reviewer

Shyam Sankar S

Acquisition Editor

Bansari Barot

Technical Editor

Dhiraj Chandiramani

Editorial Team Leader

Akshara Aware

Project Manager

Abhijeet Deobhakta

Project Coordinator

Abhijeet Deobhakta

Indexer

Monica Ajmera

Proofreader

Petula Wright

Production Coordinator

Shantanu Zagade

Cover Work

Shantanu Zagade

About the Authors

Malhar Barai is a senior systems analyst with Satyam Computer Services Ltd., one of India's leading IT services organizations. He has more than seven years of experience in the industry working for leading organizations across India.

Malhar has interest in service-oriented technologies and application integration tools. He has worked on EAI toolset of webMethods and Cast Iron, Java technologies.

You can catch him on various forums that deal with SOA and some of the webMethods forums, or you can read about him on his blog `http://malharbarai.blogspot.com`

He gets spurred by the daily challenges at work, finding solutions to the problems, and trying his hand at improving processes and solutions.

> I would like to acknowledge and dedicate this book to my parents for being sources of inspiration and for guiding me on the right path when it mattered the most. To Jalpa, my lovely wife for, being a constant support and carving out a wonderful life for us. My ex-manager Ajay Mulkalwar for his guidance and encouragement, and the most important person — my soul, my sweet daughter Preisha whose lovely smile makes my time wonderful…

Vincenzo Caselli graduated with a degree in electrical engineering in 1991 from the University of Bologna. He has worked as an independent consultant and a Java trainer for several Italian software houses since 1996. He began working as a developer in Delphi and other visual IDE's with AS/400-based companies. Soon he shifted his focus on Java and began to propose Swing client/server multi-layered solutions to his customers. He also worked in the web development area with several frameworks (Struts, Hibernate, Spring, JSF, and GWT) in different fields (banking, manufacturing, healthcare, e-learning). Recently, he collaborated with IBM in projects based on Eclipse RCP and SOA. He is interested in consultancy and training activities aimed to improve the productivity and quality of the software development process by using open-source products.

I would like to thank my wife Silvia and my daughter Linda for being patient while I worked on this book. I also want to thank my friend Luca Masini for his precious technical advice and help.

Binildas C. A. provides Technical Architecture consultancy for IT solutions. He has more than 13 years of IT experience, mostly in Microsoft and Sun technologies. Distributed Computing and Service Oriented Integration are his mainstream skills, with extensive hands-on experience in Java and C#.NET programming. Binil holds a Bachelor of Technology degree in mechanical engineering from the College of Engineering, Trivandrum (www.cet.ac.in) and an MBA in systems management from Institute of Management, Kerala (www.imk.ac.in). A well-known and a highly sought-after thought leader, Binil has designed and built many highly scalable middle-tier and integration solutions for several top-notch clients including Fortune 500 companies. He has been previously employed by multiple IT consulting firms including IBS Software Services (www.ibsplc.com) and Tata Consultancy Services (www.tcs.com), and he currently works for Infosys Technologies (www.infosys.com) as a Principal Architect where he heads the J2EE Architects group servicing Communications Service Provider clients.

Binil is a Sun Certified Programmer (SCJP), Developer (SCJD), Business Component Developer (SCBCD) and Enterprise Architect (SCEA), Microsoft Certified Professional (MCP), and Open Group (TOGAF8) Certified Enterprise Architecture Practitioner. He is also a Licensed Zapthink Architect (LZA) in SOA. Besides Technical Architecture, Binil also practices Enterprise Architecture.

When not in software, Binil spends time with wife Sowmya and daughter Ann in 'God's Own Country', Kerala (www. en.wikipedia.org/wiki/Kerala). Binil is a long distance runner and is a national medalist in power lifting. You may contact Binil at biniljava@yahoo.co.in or binil_christudas@infosys.com.

About the Reviewer

Shyam Sankar S is currently working as a Technical Architect with Allianz Cornhill Information Services, Trivandrum. He has around 11 years of experience in the IT industry and has worked in companies like IBS, Verizon, and Infosys. He has been working on Java technologies since 1999 and has been the lead architect for many JEE systems. Shyam, an Industrial Engineer from the University of Kerala, is also a Sun Certified Enterprise Architect and a Sun Certified Java Developer.

Table of Contents

Preface

Service Oriented Architecture is mainly a mindset, an enterprise strategy whose natural implementation is represented by web services. SOA is not a single product or single reference architecture to be followed, but SOA is all about best practices, reference architectures, processes, toolsets, and frameworks, along with many other things which will help you and your organization to increase the responsiveness and agility of your enterprise architecture. Standards and frameworks play a greater role in enabling easy and widespread industry adoption of SOA.

This book will help you learn the importance of designing a sound architecture for successful implementation of any business solution, different types of C/S architecture, and various tenets of SOA, explaining the fundamentals and explaining the advantage of using the Service Oriented Architecture in designing of the business solution. From a basic XML-over-HTTP approach to the REST and SOAP protocols, we get into the details of how web services can be implemented with various degrees of complexity and flexibility using JAVA.

This book will explain the concepts of business layer that is 'The SOA core'. You will also learn when SOA will define as an asset to your project with the help of practical examples.

In the early years when the WS-approach began to emerge it suffered from difficulties due to many factors, for instance, complex adoption process and poor standardization. Now, with little effort times are mature for using this technology and also getting great advantages, both immediate and as an investment for our future works. The book concludes with the focus on explanation of these assets.

What This Book Covers

In *Chapter 1* we will discuss the role of Architecture for successful implementation of any business solution followed by brief discussion on different types of client-server architecture and SOA.

In *Chapter 2* we will examine the relationship between the SOA methodology and the web service implementation basics. We will also discuss how XML can be used as the common language to decouple the communication between web service implementations and their consumer clients.

In *Chapter 3* we will introduce major web service implementations available specifically in the Java and J2EE world, WS using JAX-WS 2.0, WS using Apache Axis, WS using Spring, and WS using XFire.

In *Chapter 4* we shall see few emerging standards like SDO and SCA, addressing from data integration to service and component integration.

In *Chapter 5* we will look into a couple of case studies where one of the solutions is based on principles of Enterprise Application Integration and in the second one we shall build our solution based on SOA fundamentals.

In *Chapter 6* we will explore in detail the advantages that the SOA approach can lead to. Basically a concluding chapter discussing what we can and what we have achieved with SOA approach.

Conventions

In this book, you will find a number of styles of text that distinguish between different kinds of information. Here are some examples of these styles, and an explanation of their meaning.

There are three styles for code. Code words in text are shown as follows: "On the other hand, having a filled item into the response is meaningful just for the findById method."

A block of code will be set as follows:

```
public interface IHello{
    String sayHello (String name);
}
```

When we wish to draw your attention to a particular part of a code block, the relevant lines or items will be made bold:

```
@XmlRootElement(name="ItemAction")
public class ItemAction{
  private String method;
  private Item item;
  . . .
@XmlRootElement(name="ItemActionResponse")
public class ItemActionResponse {
  private String retCode
  private Item item;
  . . .
```

New terms and **important words** are introduced in a bold-type font. Words that you see on the screen, in menus or dialog boxes for example, appear in our text like this: "clicking the **Next** button moves you to the next screen".

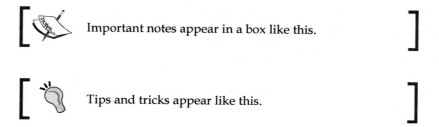

Important notes appear in a box like this.

Tips and tricks appear like this.

Reader Feedback

Feedback from our readers is always welcome. Let us know what you think about this book, what you liked or may have disliked. Reader feedback is important for us so that we may develop titles that you get the most out of.

To send us general feedback, simply drop an email to feedback@packtpub.com, making sure to mention the book title in the subject of your message.

If there is a book that you need and would like to see us publish, please send us a note in the **SUGGEST A TITLE** form on www.packtpub.com or email suggest@packtpub.com.

If there is a topic that you have expertise in and you are interested in either writing or contributing to a book, see our author guide on www.packtpub.com/authors.

Customer Support

Now that you are the proud owner of a Packt book, we have a number of things to help you to get the most from your purchase.

Downloading the Example Code for the Book

Visit `http://www.packtpub.com/files/code/3216_Code.zip` to directly download the example code.

The downloadable files contain instructions on how to use them.

Errata

Although we have taken every care to ensure the accuracy of our contents, mistakes do happen. If you find a mistake in one of our books—maybe a mistake in text or code—we would be grateful if you would report this to us. By doing this you can save other readers from frustration, and help to improve subsequent versions of this book. If you find any errata, report them by visiting `http://www.packtpub.com/support`, selecting your book, clicking on the **let us know** link, and entering the details of your errata. Once your errata are verified, your submission will be accepted and the errata are added to the list of existing errata. The existing errata can be viewed by selecting your title from `http://www.packtpub.com/support`.

Questions

You can contact us at `questions@packtpub.com` if you are having a problem with some aspect of the book, and we will do our best to address it.

1
The Mantra of SOA

Today, we are living in a world, where 'the age of information technology' is erasing the boundaries of cities, states, and countries. This age is all about M and A's and key to the success of such partnerships would depend on how well current independent resources of each of these entities is re-used. But the biggest challenge would be aligning these independent solutions into components that can be re-used across the enterprise.

The answer lies in "architecting" a design that would take care of inter-enterprise communication in a scalable form. But before getting into that, let's first try to understand the term 'architecture' in the broader sense. This is one of the most under-valued but the most important building block for any solution.

Architecture

"Architecture" is a Holy Grail for any design solution. It shows the major components of the software solution and serves as a blueprint for the entire design. It is like a core to the design of complex software solution.

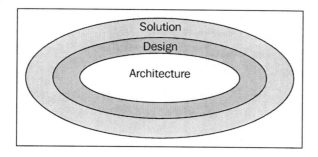

It can be defined as a representation group(s) of relationship between various components of a complex software solution. The solution is decomposed into smaller, self-describing components and represented as structural relationships to provide a high-level overview of the entire system. The system is divided into runtime elements, which in itself could have architecture as well.

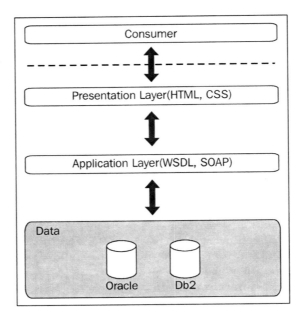

Shown here is a typical architecture for a database driven, web-based solution. It provides us with a high-level overview of the entire system. The consumer only has a view of the 'presentation layer' and other layers are tightly encapsulated. Each layer would have its own characteristics as well as its own architecture.

Architecture can be compounded as a logical set of decisions to describe the life of the project. These decisions will have a cascading affect on the selection and integration of components such as the selection of software, hardware, and behavior of the system. A good architecture will also take care of the future needs of the project.

But then, why is architecture so important? Without proper architecture in place, it would be difficult to achieve the following:

- Achieve our designed goal
- Decompose our requirements into smaller entities
- Quality solutions

- Change management
- Re-usable or extendable solutions
- Achieve business goals

Moving on from architecture, we will now dive into different architecture paradigms.

Application Architecture

At the most granular level in a system, you will always find sets of applications running to achieve some business goals. These applications are developed using different kinds of blueprints that we refer to as architecture. They provide an abstract view of the entire application, or let us say a high-level overview of the system.

Application architecture can be considered as a representation of the structure of components and the interaction between them in the system. They provide a framework within which the business objectives are represented.

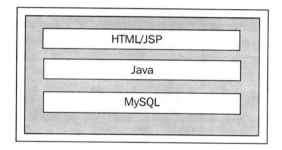

The previous figure shows a typical architecture of a web-based application. The business requirements are converted into a high-level design where the:

- First layer of 'HTML or JSP' acts as the presentation layer.
- The business logic is encapsulated in the middle layer that could be built on Servlets or EJB.
- Finally, the data is handled in the third layer 'MySQL'

Each organization will have multiple application architectures, which would cater to the need of different business goals. These applications could be web–based, or even the custom client server applications.

Client-Server Architecture

The client-server architecture also known as two-tier architecture separates the client from the server. Client is the system requesting a service from the provider (in our case, server). The client will always initiate the request, which the server processes and responds to. The client could send the request to one or more than one server at a time.

Using this architecture, you can divide the responsibilities of the requester from the provider. Earlier, as seen in monolithic systems, objectives were divided into smaller pieces, and then tightly coupled into an application. Due to this, it was difficult to process multiple clients. But, with the client-server architecture in place, business process is done within the provider. This enables multiple clients to be plugged in at the same time.

Large organizations usually have more than one application to support their business goals. These are well supported by mainframes. Mainframes act as the core business-processing unit with capacity to handle large chunks of data transactions. Other computers in the organizations access the mainframe to achieve the business goals. So in a way, the mainframes act as a server, and cater to different clients across the organization. With the advent of monolithic computing, where applications were tied to the data sources, the client-server architecture had become a welcome sign for the industry.

The main advantage of the client-server architecture is that it is scalable. With minimal performance impact, either the client or the server could be added.

Client-server architecture can be divided further into 1, 2, 3….n-tier architecture. We will glance through each of these. The architecture is made up of three basic layers — the presentation layer, the business layer, and the database or services layer.

Presentation layer is the one with which the client will interact. The consumer shall either move through a click-based solution, or will input data into the front-end to initiate the business process.

This layer could either be a thin or a fat client.

Business layer will enumerate the consumer action(s) and process the information supplied by the 'presentation layer' to accomplish a business goal with a set of business rules.

Data layer stores the data and logic that would be used to successfully achieve business goals.

1-Tier Application

The single tier application would have the three layers, that is, the presentation, the business, and the data layer tightly coupled which runs out of a single processing unit. The application is designed in a way that the interaction between the layers is interwoven.

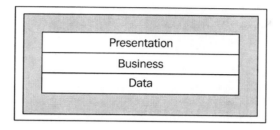

Within the tenets of client-server architecture, the single tier application can share the data layer in a multi-user environment and achieve the client-server capabilities. The limitations of 1-tier application in client-server architecture are as follows:

- Changes to the database, in case it is being edited by multiple users
- Difficulty in scalability, as the application is running on a single machine.

2-Tier Application

Within the 2-tier application, the presentation and the business layer combine on the client side, while the data layer acts as the server. This enables the business logic to be separated from the data services.

The 2-tier application would generally consist of a 'fat' client and a 'thin' server – 'fat' client because it will embed the presentation as well as the business logic of the application, and a 'thin' server, as it will only cater to the data needs of the client.

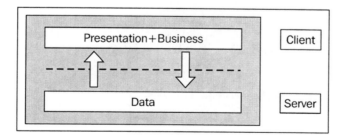

Another flavor of the 2-tier application can be a 'thin' client and a 'fat' server. This would have the presentation logic served in the 'client'. The business logic and data logic reside on the 'server'.

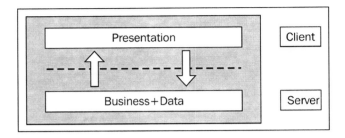

As the business logic was independent of the presentation logic, it enabled different forms of GUI to connect to a particular business process. The GUI would be served as a simple HTML application, or it could be any form of complex presentation logic.

3-Tier Application

Within a 3-tier application, the business layer would reside between the presentation layer and the data layer. This enables the presentation logic to be independent of the data layer, and all its communication will happen through the business layer only.

The business layer is usually multi-threaded so that multiple clients can access the business process. Typically, these business processes take up client calls, convert them to database queries, and then call the data layer. Subsequently, it will translate the response from the data layer and pass it to the presentation layer.

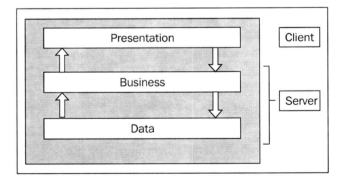

The critical advantages of the 3-tier application are:

- The business layer can be multithreaded, which enables multiple clients to access the business functions.
- Enables the presentation layer to be light weight, as it does not have to take care of the database queries.
- The components in each layer are re-usable.
- Each of the layers is easily scalable. Thus, it enables load balancing and clustering.

N-Tier application

An n-tier application will usually have more layers than the 3-tier application. Typically, the business logic from the middle layer would get structured in two different layers. Some part of the business logic will reside in the application server that connects to the data layer and the other part of the business logic shall remain in a web server, which will connect to the presentation layer.

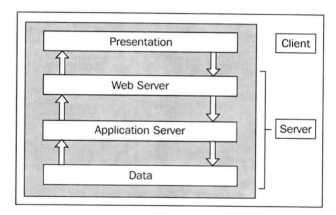

In a typical web-based solution, the client will have access to the business through a browser. The browser in turn will call the business logic in the web-server. The web server will subsequently transfer the calls to the application server, which effectively sends the request to the data layer.

Advantages of having n-tier application:

- N-tier application will offer the advantages of distributed computing.
- Each of the tiers can reside in a different system.
- The division of labor would help in reducing load from each of the tiers.
- Higher code maintainability can be achieved, which will reduce the number of errors.

Enterprise Computing or Architecture

Initially, solutions were designed to achieve certain set of goals only within the organization. Those solutions were usually built on the principles of local client-server architecture, that is, 2-tier or 3-tier architecture. But for large organizations with growing businesses that spanned across geographical locations, the localized solutions started to get redundant. A need was felt to design solutions that could interact with each other, independent of any geographical boundaries. These solutions had to be multi-tiered. In this context, we have to talk about the term 'enterprise computing'.

A large organization—with several functional entities such as HRD, Sales, Marketing, IT, and Finance—is known as 'enterprise' in the computer industry parlance. Each of these entities have their own set of business goals to achieve through different software solutions.

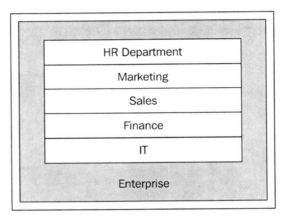

'Enterprise Computing' design makes it possible for these functional units to run on shared environment and infrastructure. It enables each of the units to share common data within the organization as well as with its trading partner.

The architecture used to design solution based on enterprise computing is 'enterprise architecture'. This architecture helps organizations achieve business goals. At a higher level, enterprise architecture can be divided into four layers:

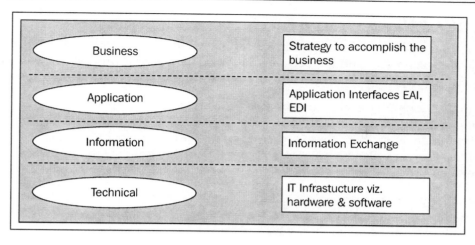

Business

The first step to evolve good enterprise architecture is to model the business processes that are directly dependent upon the business strategy.

Business logic can be set up as follows:

1. Capture business requirements
2. Analyze requirements
3. Define business strategy around the requirements
4. Model the process

The business requirement are captured and documented. The next step would be to involve different business line managers, analyze the requirements, and then define business strategies to achieve the goals as stated in the requirement document. Finally, the business process model is designed to give an overall view of the entire business process. It can be achieved through various **business process model (BPM)** tools.

Let's take a contextual example of a local super store. The store caters to the consumers through different business lines such as retail, procurement, HR, and IT. Each of these service lines is inter-dependant. To retail a product, the procurement has to be done. To procure a product, it has to be ordered, and to order a product people are needed. The business process has to be designed considering all these entities.

Application

Application will be needed in the organization to supply information to the business. Application serves as a bridge between data and the business processes. To support business goals, processes retrieve information through proprietary applications.

The applications are developed using their own reference architecture. This architecture provides a view of the processes that would be defined during the application development. These processes have a clear demarcation of their activities. For example, the process to retrieve the data would be different from the process to push the data to business.

Continuing from the super-store example we stated earlier, each of the business lines within the store will have its own applications. These applications will in turn communicate between themselves as well as use the information to achieve their individual business goals. For instance, if a product has reached the re-order level, business process are built to re-order the product. This process will use the application to check the current quantity and the re-order. In case the product is sold, it will reduce the quantity.

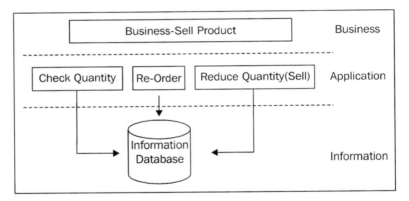

Information

Just as a fish cannot live without water, an enterprise solution cannot exist without information. Information is the critical building block to any enterprise solution. It constitutes a major part of the solution, which the enterprise architect has to take into consideration:

- Data redundancy
- Data re-use
- Access control
- Regular backups

These checks help in maintaining the accuracy of data for business processes.

Technical

The success of any enterprise solution will depend upon the appropriate technical decisions. Implementation of applications and the use of information will depend upon the type of technical components being utilized.

The choice of hardware and software components will depend upon the current infrastructure assets, and the correct alignment of the components in the business processes. Traditional 3GL languages are still used in bigger enterprises where performance is as critical as the business. But the new world prefers to use the 4GL languages.

The Design

The enterprise systems are designed in a way that all the business goals can be shared by all the consumers, and at the same time it does remain abstract. The sharing of info could be done with various supporting interfaces. For example, where data needs to be exchanged, it can be done through XML interfaces. These data can also be referenced through HTML or other UI systems.

Moving to 'enterprise computing' designs, the organization started to reap good profits. Let's list the advantages of 'enterprise computing':

- Information is exchanged over network(s).
- It enables the concept of 'paperless' office, as all communication can be routed over the internet, thus removing the dependence on standard mail, fax, or even email.
- Man-hours, consumed to do the menial tasks, are reduced.
- The collaborative mechanism approach enables better and faster supply-chain management
- The turnaround time for moving the product from the manufacturing hub to the store is vastly reduced.

- Data between each of the units can be exchanged faster, greatly reducing the cost-to-carry.

Security

Now, when we talk about data exchange, the major hiccup comes in the form of security. The sensitive data exchange has to be accomplished in a secure environment, as the networks are open to intruders most of the times. This could cause immeasurable losses to the enterprises. Security can be achieved through various means such as using secured HTTP protocols, authentication, and proper logging mechanism. It can help to catch leaks and send appropriate notifications, access controls, or enable only a set of users to access the resources.

Administration

Further, with the growth in size of enterprise solutions, the need for administration became very important. As the enterprise grew, so did the number of software and hardware components. Any errors or inherent bug in the solution need careful debugging and resolution process.

Many times, the software components would require an upgrade, which spanned across the multitudes of business lines. So, application administration was required to ease the task of upgrades and timely resolution of errors.

EA for Managers

The managers have a fair idea of the business process and the need for improvement in various solutions. They are the people who run the business and are single-handedly responsible for the continuous improvement of the system. These improvement needs are guided by the goal to achieve continuous high quality growth in each of the business systems.

To achieve it, managers always need to have an overview of the enterprise system, which can be achieved by involving the managers during the design of the solutions. The managers can get involved in the design with their inputs on the business goals, and help to set up business rules to achieve these goals. These would be helpful in case a system needed improvements, or while debugging any inherent issues.

Managers who are aware of the enterprise architecture give a greater fillip to the organizations to achieve better quality and consistent growth, as they can relate the architecture to the business goals better, using the data gained out of the system. They can design various metrics out of the data to analyze the growth and address any impediments in achieving their targets.

EA for Developers

For developers, architecture is a ready resource to the way they understand the business requirements. Successful enterprise solutions are a derivative of good enterprise architecture. Depending on this understanding of the architecture, decisions are made by the developers on:

- Development milestones
- Development strategies
- Choice of proprietary software solution
- Choice of hardware
- Choice of manpower (for the technical leads)

A perfect blend of the above will result in the successful implementation of enterprise solution vis-à-vis the enterprise goals.

But, EA solutions had its share of challenges. We will try to discuss some of the common challenges faced by the organizations that were dependent on enterprise architecture techniques to accomplish their business goals:

1. **Proprietary Solutions**: With the organization's business horizon growing, it had to incorporate EA solutions that were traditionally being delivered through proprietary software, or there was a wide use of proprietary software either on the side of the organization, or its vendors. This led to many more challenges in the dissemination of data between the concerned parties, which ended up impacting the business goals and delivery timelines.

2. **Point-to-Point Integration**: EA solutions required applications within the organization to communicate with vendor application for the exchange of data without any human intervention. This required business process to make a one-to-one connection with the vendor-side process.

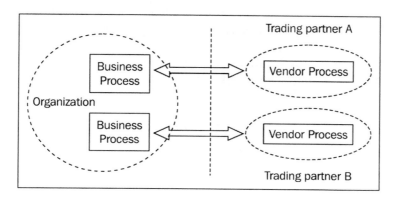

Problems with Point-to-Point integration:

- For large organizations, an increase in number of point-to-point interface leads to chaotic maintenance issues.
- It becomes difficult to re-use organizational business processes as they are tightly coupled with vendor process.
- It requires dedicated hardware connections to the vendor.
- The ROI declines over the long term, because when each client is added, the hardware and software connections have to be made. This increases the infrastructure costs in the long term, as the number of vendors increase.
- Only one-way communication is possible including messaging. Suppose the message sent by Vendor process has to be propagated to the other vendor system, in this case a new solution will have to be set up and maintained.

3. **Technology**: New technologies are arriving at a fast pace, and all of them want to market themselves as the best solution providers. But this is the place where organizations are thrown a lot of challenges. Although the new technology will reduce the time to implement the business processes, organizations have to estimate how it could affect the current processes. They have to choose between upgradating and investment in the current systems, or maintenance of the existing systems.

   The cascading effect is seen in business processes that interact with trading partners. With the change in technology of the business processes on either side, the information flow and connections have to be reset. This will need investment in the form of man-hours and, in some cases, additional hardware resources.

4. **Standards**: Business processes being tightly coupled to the vendor processes, information exchange follows a set of agreed standards between the two. This leads to less openness and re-use of information. The challenge is to convert the organization's meaning of a data item to various vendors' data item. A shipping order should not be conceived differently between the two vendors. A common standard for information exchange has to be set up, which would translate the meaning across vendors.

5. **Mergers and Acquisitions**: With rapid globalization, many organizations are looking for opportunities to expand their businesses. So mergers and acquisitions have become the order of the day. But for IT, these have become one of the major challenges. There is a high need for either revamping the current processes, or setting up additional infrastructure to develop new offerings. There is a constant lack of cohesiveness between the business processes, and the advantage of shared growth is lost. This loss can be seen in multiple solutions for the same set of business processes such as in a shipping order or a simple login mechanism.

This can have an effect on the business of the organizations. In the long term, strategies have to be realigned to take advantage of the fast-paced growth. Open standards have to be set by organizations, so that information can be exchanged more easily. These will help in tiding over the current set of challenges offered by EA. Organizations need newer strategies for:

- Faster time to market
- Meeting information exchange challenges
- Loose coupling between the business processes
- Re-use of infrastructure

For organizations that are truly bent on developing new strategies to achieve their renewed set of goals, here comes SOA to their rescue.

Analogy of SOA

"We are building business processes around web services in our solution. So, we're essentially developing a SOA-based solution". Well, this is the common perception across the ranks within the organization, and at times even the architect would say it. But is that really so?

Well, in our opinion, that's not true. Just because you are using web services, it would be unfair to classify it as a SOA-based solution. So, what exactly constitutes SOA? This has become a focal point in the various discussions that we're involved in during our day-to-day life. Defining SOA is a challenge in itself. In a nutshell, we need to understand that SOA is an architectural concept. To understand our point of view on SOA, let us first go through web services and the 'orientation' of web services.

Web Services for SOA

With the aim of re-using the business processing logic, and moving away from point-to-point communication, a need was felt by organizations to promote information across vendors. They were required to communicate over the web, using a set of standards. So, processes were set up to be accessed over the web to execute the business logic.

The communication was independent of the underlying technologies on either side. Use of web services eliminates the issues of application servers, operating systems, protocols, or devices. Regardless of the above, vendors can call the web service to accomplish a set of tasks.

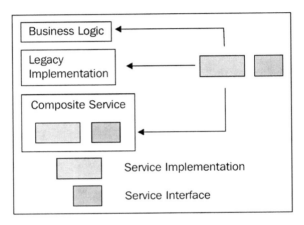

'Orientation' of Web Services

We have been hearing about object-orientation for a long time. Extending the concepts further, we try to explain the 'orientation' of web services. In a nutshell, it is an enterprise solution with a plethora of business processes exposed as web service. But each of this process has to be defined according to the business goals they are supposed to achieve. Orientation is the process of mapping the business processes, and enabling them to conform to the business goals.

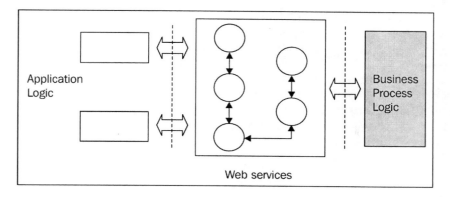

Web services

The web services expose the business process and communicate with the Application logic to accomplish a business task. These web services can be accessed within and outside the organization.

We will go into the details of each of these in the *'Why SOA?'* section.

History of SOA

SOA is not a solution, it is a practice.

The term SOA was first coined by Gartner analyst Yefim V. Natis in one of the research papers in 1994. According to Yefim:

SOA is a software architecture that starts with an interface definition and builds the entire application topology as a topology of interfaces, interface implementations, and interface calls...

Despite being coined much earlier, SOA started to become a buzzword only in early 2000. With the advent of web services and WSDL compliant business process, SOA started to become popular among technology enthusiasts.

The SOA Bandwagon

The fundamental of SOA is based upon:

- Service
- Message
- Dynamic discovery
- Web service

The fundamental approach of designing web services that offered the business logic to be decomposed amongst disparate services, each of which was a distinct logical unit but in entirety was part of a distributed enterprise solution. These logical units are services.

The business logic gets encapsulated in a service. As seen earlier, a service can be an independent logical unit or it can contain in itself other set of services, as shown in figure 1. In case the service is used to call other sets of dependant services, to refer to those services, they must contain the *service descriptions*. The service description in its basic form contains the information of service name and location of the service being called.

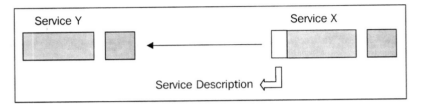

These logical units though had to adhere to certain sets of communication standards to enable information flow across the enterprise offerings in an understandable form. The information is exchanged in the form of messages from the interface designed within the system. The interface exposed by a service contains the service behavior and messaging pattern. One of the basis of SOA being platform-neutral is that messages are exchanged in XML formats so as to adhere to the concept.

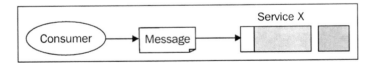

At a high level, SOA is formed out of three core components:

- Service Provider (Service)
- Service Consumer (Consumer)
- Directory Services (enabled by Broker)

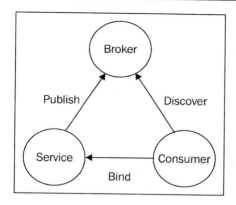

From the preceding figure, we can see that:

- The service provider offers business processes in the form of services.
- The services offered by the provider are called by the consumer to achieve certain sets of business goals.
- The process of services being provided and consumed is achieved by using directory services that lie between the provider and the consumer, in the form of broker.

The service to be made available to the consumer is published to the directory services in the broker. The consumer wanting to achieve the set of business goal(s) will discover the service from the broker. If the service is found, it will bind to the service and execute the processing logic.

This helps in achieving the objective of using SOA:

- **Loose coupling**: The business process being decomposed into independent services will help in bringing down the dependencies on a single process. This in turn will help in faster processing time.
- **Platform-neutrality**: XML-based message information flow enhances the capability to achieve platform neutrality. These XML messages are based on agreed XML schema, eliminating the need to set up other messaging standards that can differ across platforms.

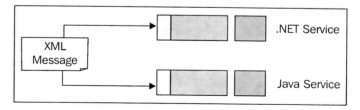

- **Standards**: The message flow across the enterprise is in the form of globally accepted standards. The service only has to depend on the service descriptions without worrying about the target standards and removing the dependencies.

- **Reusability**: The business logic being divided into smaller logical units, the services can easily be re-used. These enhance the utilization of SOA-based solution, which has a cascading affect on service delivery and execution.

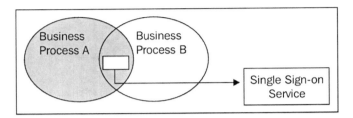

- **Scalability**: Again, as the business processes are decomposed into smaller units, adding new business logic is easy to accomplish. The new logic could either be added as an extended unit of the current service, or it can also be constructed as a new service.

Why SOA?

We have discussed above the concepts of SOA and the components that constitute the design of architecture based on service orientation. In this section, we'll try to determine the need for organizations to align their business process, and design it according to service-oriented concepts, joining the SOA wagon wheel.

- **Integration**: An SOA-based solution is usually based upon the principles of inter-operability. The integration solutions thus offered are loosely coupled and less complex. At the granular level, services are being used to interact with vendors. The compounded benefit can be found in the lower cost of integration development, as we move away from proprietary integrations solutions to open standard-based solutions.

  The ROI can be easily measured for integration solutions as the cost per integration is drastically reduced by the use of SOA-based solution against the traditional middleware solutions. Over the period of time, organizations can move away from the current, expensive, integration solutions to SOA-based vendor-neutral integration standards. It can be achieved by standardizing the current service description and messaging solutions.

- **Business Agility**: One of the most important benefits of organizations adopting SOA is felt by the increased agility within the systems. Though agility is a non-quantifiable term, the inherent benefit is felt within the organization's hardware and software assets.

  The benefit in terms of software assets can be derived from SOA's ability to re-use and simplify integrations. Unlike earlier days, where development of new business process would take quite some time, the current business users will find the development period getting shortened. This makes it easy to accommodate changes, and the benefits of the same can be seen in the long term, as the enterprise solution evolves over a period of time.

  In terms of hardware benefits, due to the abstract use of services being loosely coupled, they can be delegated across the domain and the results can still be achieved. This helps in balancing the business processes load across the organization, and the capabilities can be utilized better. Thus, a remarkable improvement in the efficiency of business can be felt.

- **Assets Re-use**: The foremost goal of a SOA-based solution is 're-use'. Most of the earlier solutions were built-in a very tightly coupled or an isolated environment. This made it very difficult to re-use the components of the current solution.

  SOA-based services were built in such a manner that, though the services conformed to the current business requirement, they could still be re-used in any composite service. As a result, organizations saw the benefits of re-use in terms of a higher intial development period. But over time, the economics of re-use got better of the development span. The economics of re-use was felt in terms of faster integration and lower cost per integrations. Re-use also enabled organization to put less money into asset growth, as the current assets were being re-used effectively.

- **Increased ROI**: With proper governance and compliance in place, and a highly secured transaction environment, the adoption of SOA sees a definite increase in terms of ROI.

  With the integration solutions moving from expensive, tightly coupled, standard-specific, vendor dependent to being loosely coupled, vendor-neutral, open standard-based solutions, the cascading effect on ROI is seen immediately. Over time, as organizations move away from proprietary solutions to SOA-based solutions, the investment in integration assets will surely dwindle.

  Building solutions that are inherently re-usable helps organizations to build and market the solutions in a rapid manner. This helps organizations to improve their time-to-market, and improve efficiency with respect to customer satisfaction, service, and effective use of manpower.

How SOA...

As a lot of organizations move towards adopting the SOA culture, the biggest issue faced by them is the complexity of the solutions. The dismantling of the current business processes into smaller services is a huge challenge in itself. SOA is a natural improvement over the **object-oriented (OO)** and the **component-based development (CBD)**. So, it still retains some of the flavors from each of them.

The business processes are powered by small pieces of software known as 'components'. The business logic inside the components is based on the principles of OO programming. These business processes are termed as 'services' in the analogy of SOA.

The recipe for success of any SOA solution is to ensure the classification of business processes into smaller units. You can either choose the top-down, the bottom-up, or the middle-out approach.

- **Top-down**: In a top-down approach, the business use cases are created, which gives the specifications for the creation of services. This would ensure that the functional units are decomposed into smaller processes and then developed.
- **Bottom-up**: Using the bottom-up approach, the current systems within the organization are studied, and suitable business processes are identified for conversion to services.
- **Middle-out**: The middle-out approach acts as a spy, and tries to locate suitable business processes that were left out by the other two approaches.

Service

From the above discussions, we can identify that 'services' are the core components for the success of a SOA-based solution. We will try to explain the term in the following discussion.

'Service' as a sole unit is an independent logical unit of a business process. The business logic stands encapsulated into the service, and it interacts with the outer world through the 'interface'. The services are designed to be flexible in terms of addition of new business logic or change of logic. They should also be reusable, so that other processes can use functionality. Services are published by the 'provider' and they bind to the 'consumer' through the service 'handler'.

- **The Service provider**: The provider comes into action when the service is invoked. Once the service is invoked, the provider will execute the business logic. Messaging will depend upon the business logic, in case the consumer expects a message after the execution of business process, the provider will send out the reply.

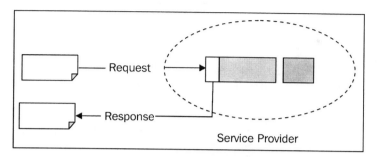

- **The Service Consumer**: The consumer would send out a message to the provider in order to access the service. This is the requester. It would either be done directly by a service-to-service call or through the directory services. Services required for processing are identified by their service descriptions.

  The same service can act as the provider as well as the requester of the service. But this is seldom seen in practice. Here, we have extended the above image further:

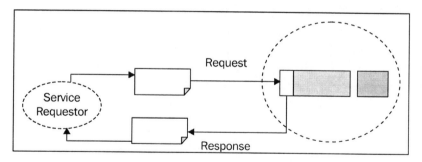

- **The Service Handler**: The service handler acts as a collaboration agent between the provider and the consumer. The handler contains the realization logic, which will search the appropriate service provided and bind it to the consumer request.

Once the service has been requested, it goes through various messaging paths and, at times, into multiple handlers to finally accomplish the logic. The handler usually routes the messages to the target system or sometimes does some processing logic before forwarding the request to target system.

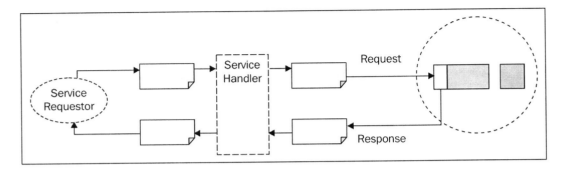

- **WSDL—Service Description**: Service Description carries information about the service such as the input or output parameter, the location of the service, port type, binding information, and so on.

This helps in locating the service when a consumer requests for the same. This information is stored in the form of a **WSDL (Web Service Definition Language)** document. In a nutshell, the WSDL document will have all the information needed by the consumer to locate and execute the business logic within the web service.

The WSDL can be classified in two different entities: abstract and concrete. The abstract definition constitutes port and messages, whereas the concrete definition will constitute the binding, port, and service information.

The messages are structured within the **XSD (XML Schema Definition)** and processing rules are defined as part of policy within the WSDL.

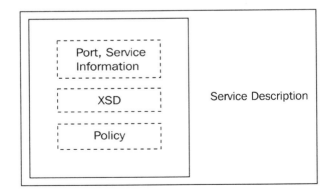

Messaging

Messaging in the SOA paradigm is one of the most important blocks. The inter-service and inter-vendor sharing of information is done through messages. SOA-based solutions have an exhaustive usage of messages. The messages are designed in an agreed upon standard format to be used by services across the SOA-based solution.

SOAP is the standard messaging protocol agreed upon by the industry as a means of sharing information over networks. The information is stored in the form of XML data within SOAP.

SOAP specification consists of:

- Envelope
- Header
- Body

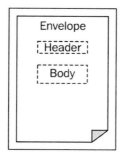

Each SOAP message will consist of an envelope, header, and a body. The header will contain information about the SOAP message and all the metadata required by the message. This is, however, an optional element in the SOAP envelope.

The body contains the actual message required for execution of the web service at the endpoints. The message conforms to the XML standards. The body also includes information about faults—a way of error handling. A message can be added in case an error occurs while processing. This field is also optional.

As part of the messaging framework, enterprise solution uses nodes for SOAP messages to communicate across the platform.

Nodes

SOAP nodes are supposed to perform the processing logic on receiving a SOAP message. The node is identified by an URI.

The nodes can be:

- The SOAP intermediary
- The sender of the SOAP message
- The initiator of SOAP message

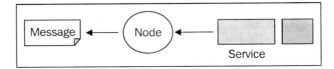

RPC Style

One of the most common messaging styles is the **RPC (Remote Procedure Call)** mechanism. It enables developers to make a call to the remote services over the HTTP.

For making RPC call, the payload within the envelope will represent the method call. In the conventional way, the method name will be used for request and the responses come in the form of "Response" being appended to the name– for example, PurchRequest or PurchRequestResponse.

Message Path

It is the path taken by the message from the moment it was initiated by the request till it reaches the target service.

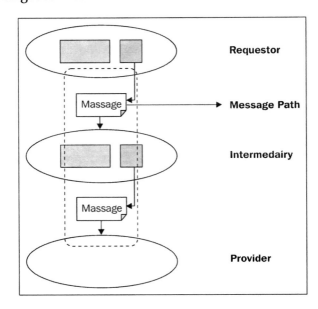

The path starts from the service requester and moves towards the logical end of the service. Message Path is important, as it will determine the flow of service and address the concern of security, data management, and service management.

Many times, the message path is not pre-determined, and would depend upon the number of intermediaries between the requester and the target.

More on WSDL and messaging style will be covered in the next chapter. This way, we have addressed some of the tenets of working up on SOA.

Summary

In this chapter, we have covered:

1. **Role of Architecture**: This describes the importance of designing a sound architecture for successful implementation of any business solution.

2. **Client-Server Architecture**: Different type of client-server architecture has been offered for reference. They serve as prologue to the service-based architecture.

3. **SOA**: We have tried to cover the various tenets of SOA, explaining the fundamentals and explaining the advantage of using the service-oriented architecture in designing a business solution.

2
Web Services and SOA

In this chapter, we will get into the details of SOA implementation and start practicing in the domain of web services. We will see why XML is the right choice for exchanging messages in an enterprise interoperable environment. Then, starting from a sample set of service definitions, we will follow a top-down methodology to develop our first basic web services. The process will be refined by applying the two commonly used communication protocols (REST and SOAP).

A comparison between the two available styles of web services (RPC and Document) will then be introduced and we will see how the latter is better and widely adopted. In the last section, we will then go through a quick introduction to the most popular web service implementation frameworks.

The SOA Approach

The first step in the path to the SOA is basically the expression of a very simple approach: *identifying the business functions that your applications are made of*. Let's analyze this phrase in detail:

- **Identifying**: is the ability to find and isolate the software parts that provide self-contained and atomic functionalities. This implies designing in a modular way, that is *divide* ("et Impera", Romans would say) the logics of your problem into small and well defined call specifications. We need to build the boundaries of our software parts and contracts to use them, always keeping in mind that a part that is re-usable in many contexts is sort of a piece of gold. In a sense, we are simply leveraging the concept of "interface" to a more abstract level, the business rule's level.

- **Business functions**: refers to the fact that with SOA we are focusing on the model-and-business layer (the M letter in MVC), and not the presentation side (the View and Controller).What we are talking about here is exactly "services". A well-designed service should be *agnostic* about the specific presentations that it will serve.

- **Applications are made of**: a lot of software layers. Here, though, we want to put the emphasis on the "s" of "applications". This is the "big leap" of the SOA approach, going beyond the project we are facing just now, and making a little effort in order to build a thing that will survive the single project and will be eligible to be exploited in a wider scenario, that is, by several applications, and over time.

Now, suppose we have accepted the above methodology and we have also designed the services we need, what are the next steps? How do we implement them?

As a sample service, let's take the one which retrieves the list of all customers. That is a very simple function. It has no input parameters and returns a list of objects.

How is the service consumer (the part of software that makes use of the service, for example, on the User Interface side) expected to invoke the service and receive the list of requested objects?

This can be done in different ways. Among them, the most popular are:

- **With platform native calls**: As far as Java is concerned this may be implemented through **Remote Method Invocation (RMI)**, Sockets, Servlets, or JMS.
- **With a distributed object communication middleware**: CORBA or DCOM are just some examples.
- **With a text-based communication protocol**: This can be done by sending the request as a text stream and obtaining a textual response containing the data. This is the approach on which web services are based.

The first way is straightforward, but it has some drawbacks. It is tied to a common language (the service and its consumer must share the same technology and language—for example Java, .NET). Furthermore, the exchanged object's classes must be the same version otherwise the communication will not happen.

Distributed object communication middleware have been a successful answer for a considerable time span. CORBA in particular, thanks to its cross-platform nature, has offered an evident asset where interoperability was needed.

The text-based approach implies, on the other side, a process of serialization (conversion from object to a textual form) when the client sends the request, and a process of deserialization (conversion from text to object) when received by the server. A similar double process must happen then for the response flow.

The serialization and deserialization processes seem to add complexity to the communication. But consider the advantage, a complete independence from technologies and loose coupling between parts.

The natural way to embed data in a textual form is definitely throughout XML.

XML—Advantages and Disadvantages

The eXtensible Markup Language was designed by the **W3C** (**World Wide Web Consortium**) in 1998. It was designed exactly for data exchange purposes and has demonstrated its strength over time.

The advantages that XML provides are significant. In fact, it is:

- Structured
- Portable
- Extensible
- Text format

XML Pitfalls

The tree-based structure of XML may lead to some apparent problems. A common debate is about the fact that XML is not the best way to represent an arbitrary object because of its limitations when it comes to sharing object references. Think about the previous example. Imagine you have a number of customers in London, with the above representation you would have an overhead of redundant data (a number of identical "city" blocks), which is barely acceptable.

Indeed this example was made just to show a common misuse, where the attribute <city> should be considered as an independent **entity**, rather than a **value**.

A better approach would be to handle the problem just like you would do with a **relational database** that is moving repeated data outside of the main object and embedding just a reference to them in the latter.

With a **Stateful approach**, the client could have retrieved the list of all "city" entities at a previous stage. So when it calls the getAllCustomers service, this could return just the city ids.

Listing 1—Stateful Approach

```
<Customers>
    <customer>
        <id>4</id>
        <name>Smith Ltd</name>
        <location>
            <address>39, Kensington Rd.</address>
```

```
                <city>LND</city>
            </location>
        </customer>
        <customer>
            <id>7</id>
            <name>Merkx & Co.</name>
            <location>
                <address>39, Venice Blvd.</address>
                <city>LAX</city>
            </location>
        </customer>
        . . .
    </Customers>
```

On the other side, if we want to adopt a **Stateless approach**, in order to have a **self-contained** service, we could embed in the response of all the needed lists of data.

Listing 2—Stateless Approach

```
    <Entireresponse>
    <cities>
        <city>
          <id>LND</id>
          <name>London</name>
          <country>UK</country>
        </city>
        <city>
          <id>LAX</id>
          <name>Los Angeles</name>
          <country>USA</country>
        </city>
    </cities>

    <customers>
        <customer>
            <id>4</id>
            . . .
            <location>
            . . .
            <city>LND</city>
            </location>
        </customer>
        <customer>
            <id>7</id>
            . . .
            <location>
```

```
      . . .
      <city>LAX</city>
    </location>
  </customer>
  . . .
</customers>
    </Entireresponse>
```

Introduction to Web Services, RESTful Services, and Other Transport with XML

The previous section focused on the advantages that XML adoption brings in SOA implementation, but no mention was made of web services. The terms SOA and web services are sometimes mixed up in the same discussion at the risk of creating some misunderstanding.

SOA is just a methodology, an architectural design choice. It has nothing to do with technology or languages. In "Service Oriented Architecture", the first word is not short for "Web Service"; it is just "Service" in its wider meaning. We can design the service that retrieves the list of all items (or a subset filtered upon criteria) without being involved in the technology implementation choice.

Designing by SOA is, in the end, designing the high-level interfaces of the business rules of a given domain model.

At some point, however, an implementation choice must be made. Therefore, in this paragraph we will explore some solutions, going from a simpler home-made approach, to a complete and widely accepted standard technology (SOAP).

Before going ahead though, it is important to focus on a term that we will use very often in this book.

The term is "protocol" and as we will discover soon, it can be used with different meanings depending on the context. One crucial distinction is between "Transportation (or layer) protocol" and "Communication protocol".

The first refers to the network protocol that transports the information. It may be HTTP (a very common choice), but also may be SMTP (thus allowing asynchronous data exchange) or JMS.

Communication protocol, instead, deals with the way we put and extract the message into and from an XML document, and will be the main subject of this section.

At first, we will see how to build a very basic system where XML requests and responses are exchanged through the HTTP protocol in a homemade manner. This will help understand some communication mechanisms from the ground up.

Then, this approach will be standardized with the REST, getting to a still more basic SOA implementation, but with a clean and well designed communication protocol.

Finally, with SOAP, we will go through a more complete and flexible solution with a wide range of features.

Basic SOA With XML Over HTTP Protocol

The process of designing services yields to a number of results. First of all, it produces a list of service definitions which is sometime referred to as a "Catalog of Services". This, naturally, should not have the form of a flat list, but will be organized into sections or "Functional Domains". So we could have, for example, the "Item", "Order", and "Customer" functional domains. Under these functional domains, the following services can be defined:

Item Functional domains are as follows:

- insertItem
- updateItem
- deleteItemById
- findItemById
- findAllItems
- findItemsByCriteria

Order Functional domains are as follows:

- createOrder
- findOrderById
- findAllOrdersByCustomer

Often there will be the need for some "orthogonal" services. In fact, some services could share common mechanisms, such as a control flow or transaction handling.

Generally, at the beginning of any software design process, a common task is to focus on the basic domain objects and their essential handling operations: **Create** (or insert), **Read** (select), **Update**, and **Delete**. This is usually referred to as **CRUD**. No matter which language you are using, which architecture is adopted, all projects virtually have to deal with CRUD actions. In our case, a basic domain object is the Item entity and the first four listed services are exactly the CRUD functions.

Let's begin by analyzing and designing the services that handle the item domain. The `insertItem` service, for example, could have the following form:

Create

Input	Service	Output

`<Item>`
`    <id>0</id>`
`    <code>RX004</code>`
`    <description>`
`      Eth. Cable`
`    </description>`
`</Item>`
	=> insertItem =>	`<Result>`
		`    <retCode>`
		`      OK`
		`    </retCode>`
		`    <id>137</id>`
		`</Result>`

The client who wants to use this service in order to insert a new item must provide an XML message with the above input schema. Note that the item id has a zero value, since it is assumed that the server will assign it and return to the client along with a return code.

The other three CRUD actions could be modeled as follows:

Read

Input	Service	Output

`<ItemId>`
`    <id>137</id>`
`</ItemId>`
	=> findItemById =>	`<Item>`
		`    <id>137</id>`
		`    <code>`
		`      RX004`
		`    </code>`
		`    <description>`
		`      Eth. Cable 4 ft.`
		`    </description>`
		`</Item>`

Update

Input	Service	Output

`<Item>`
`    <id>137</id>`
`    <code>RX004</code>`
`    <description>`
`      Eth. Cable 4 ft.`
`    </description>`
`</Item>`
	=> updateItem =>	`<Result>`
		`    <retCode>`
		`      OK`
		`    </retCode>`
		`    <id>137</id>`
		`</Result>`

Delete

Input	Service	Output
```<ItemId> <id>137</id> </ItemId>```	=> deleteItem =>	```<Result> <retCode> OK </retCode> <id>0</id> </Result>```

The above design is just an example of the possible communication protocol we can adopt. In fact, in this scenario, without constraints or patterns to follow, we are free to decide the communication protocol. For example, we could find it better to have a unique input-output pattern and a single entry point for all CRUD methods. Here the input is a message with the service name embedded, along with the item object, while the output is composed by a return code and an item object, as described in the following figure.

Generic CRUD Action

Input	Service	Output
```<ItemAction> <method> findById </method> <item> <id>137</id> <code></code> <description> </description> </item> </ItemAction>```	=> itemCrudService =>	```<ItemActionResponse> <retCode>OK</retCode> <item> <id>137</id> <code>RX004</code> <description> Eth. Cable 4 ft. </description> </item> </ItemActionResponse>```

Here the advantage of having a single service for all CRUD actions has a price: we have to provide a partially filled item object (with just the id attribute valued) while invoking the service with `findById` and `delete` methods (in fact only the insert and the update methods need to really pass the full-valued item object). On the other hand, having a filled item into the response is meaningful just for the `findById` method.

However, the CRUD actions do not cover, generally, all the needed services. For instance, in the Item domain, we also need a method that retrieves all the items or at least a subset of them. A possible specification of this service could be the following:

Non-CRUD Action

Input	Service	Output
void input	=> findAllItems =>	```<Items>\n <item>\n <id>137</id>\n <code>RX004</code>\n <description>\n Eth. Cable 4 ft.\n </description>\n </item>\n . . .\n</Items>```

So far, we have explored a couple of feasible paths that the service designer may follow. As you noticed, the communication protocol is completely up to you. There are no guidelines, just your skill to abstract concepts.

Once we have settled for the communication protocol (may be one of the above or yet another of your choice), we need to think about the layer protocol and its details. The HTTP protocol is a very practical and flexible solution: we can send the XML message as an HTTP request. This approach is also known as POX-over-HTTP, where **POX** stands for **Plain Old Xml**.

In practice, we just need an XML translation library in order to transform the objects written in our programming language into XML documents and vice versa. This is all we need for implementing the services we have described above. But there is more. We can even use different languages for implementing the client and the server side as long as each layer adheres to the defined protocol. The XML document is the key to decoupling parts, as shown in the following figure, where a possible scenario is depicted:

Web Service Decoupling

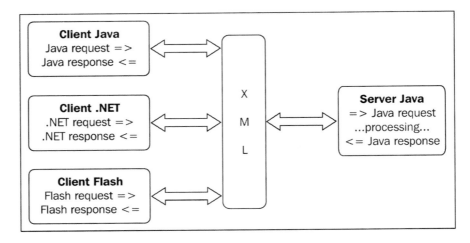

A Basic Java Implementation of POX-over-HTTP

Now, to complete the example, we will see how to implement the findById service in the Java language. For the automatic binding, we decided to use the **JAXB library**. This component is included into the latest **Java 6 JDK**. So if you use this version of Java you do not need any additional jars. Otherwise, you will have to download JAXB and add it explicitly to your server and client class paths. However, since we will make use of Java Annotations, the following source code requires at least a JDK 5 release in order to be compiled and executed. For the server side service implementation, we adopted Tomcat 5.5. The implementation we are stepping through is in fact made up of a simple Java Servlet.

Let's start with the classes that will be exchanged between the client and the server: Item, ItemAction, and ItemActionResponse. There is very little indeed to say about them; they are basic **POJO (Plain Old Java Object)** with a Java annotation that has a key role in the process of XML serialization/deserialization.

Listing 3—XML Binding Annotations

```
@XmlRootElement(name="Item")
public class Item {
    private int id;
    private String code;
    private String description;
    ... getter/setter methods omitted ...
```

```
@XmlRootElement(name="ItemAction")
public class ItemAction{
  private String method;
  private Item item;
  ...

@XmlRootElement(name="ItemActionResponse")
public class ItemActionResponse {
  private String retCode
  private Item item;
  ...
```

The following code represents our main goal: the service implementation. It is implemented in the doPost() method of a Servlet that was mapped with the url-pattern /itemCrudService in the application descriptor web.xml.

Listing 4—ItemCrudService Server Implementation

```
protected void doPost(HttpServletRequest request,
                      HttpServletResponse response)
                  throws ServletException, IOException
{
  try{
    JAXBContext jaxbContext = JAXBContext.newInstance
                       (ItemAction.class, ItemActionResponse.class);
    Unmarshaller unmarshaller = jaxbContext.createUnmarshaller();
    //Receiving the XML request and transform it into a Java object
    ItemAction itemAction = (ItemAction)
                  unmarshaller.unmarshal(request.getInputStream());
    //Do some action depending on the request content
    String method = itemAction.getMethod();
    //Prepare the response as a Java object
    ItemActionResponse itemActionResponse = new ItemActionResponse();
    if ("findById".equals(method)){
      int id = itemAction.getItem().getId();
      //Retrieve item (e.g. from db)
      Item item = new Item();
      item.setId(id);
      item.setCode("Item XYZ");
      item.setDescription("Description item XYZ");
      //Fill the response
      itemActionResponse.setRetCode("OK");
      itemActionResponse.setItem(item);
    }
    Marshaller marshaller = jaxbContext.createMarshaller();
    marshaller.setProperty(Marshaller.JAXB_FORMATTED_OUTPUT,
                           Boolean.TRUE);
    //The following line is not required, it was inserted
```

```
        //just to see the content of the generated XML message
        marshaller.marshal(itemActionResponse, System.out);
        //Send the XML message to the client
        marshaller.marshal( itemActionResponse,
                          response.getOutputStream());
    }
  catch (JAXBException e){
    throw new ServletException(e);
  }
}
```

We have just written a basic web service; the flow is clear:

1. Deserialize the XML request

2. Do the processing

3. Prepare and serialize the response

Please note that the above service can be invoked by any language or technology, as long as the process of XML serialization or deserialization is available and the communication protocol is known on the client side.

The Java code for testing the service is as follows:

Listing 5—ItemCrudService Client Request

```
//Prepare the request
ItemAction itemAction = new ItemAction();
Item item = new Item();
item.setId(26);
itemAction.setMethod("findById");
itemAction.setItem(item);
//Prepare and establish the connection with the service
URL url = new URL("http://localhost/SoaBookPoxHttp/itemCrudService");
HttpURLConnection con = (HttpURLConnection) url.openConnection();
con.setDoOutput(true);
//Set the HTTP request method
con.setRequestMethod("POST");
con.connect();
JAXBContext jaxbContext = JAXBContext.newInstance
                        (ItemAction.class, ItemActionResponse.class);
Marshaller marshaller = jaxbContext.createMarshaller();
marshaller.setProperty(Marshaller.JAXB_FORMATTED_OUTPUT,
                        Boolean.TRUE);
//The following line is not required, it was inserted
//just to see the content of the generated XML message
marshaller.marshal(itemAction, System.out);
```

```
//Send the XML request to the service
marshaller.marshal(itemAction, con.getOutputStream());

//Get the XML response from the service and deserialize it
Unmarshaller unmarshaller = jaxbContext.createUnmarshaller();
ItemActionResponse itemActionResponse = (ItemActionResponse)
                        unmarshaller.unmarshal(con.getInputStream());
//Show the response content
System.out.println("retCode="+itemActionResponse.getRetCode()+ "\r" +
                "id="+itemActionResponse.getItem().getId()+ "\r" +
                "code="+itemActionResponse.getItem().getCode()+
                "\r"+"description="+itemActionResponse.getItem()
                .getDescription());
```

As you see, on the client side, it is mandatory to have the visibility of all the classes involved in the communication process (Item, ItemAction, and ItemActionResponse). In this case, where Java is used both for service implementation and client development, these classes were just copied from the server side and dropped into the client project. In general, of course, this is not a requirement (think about using different languages). The only requirement is having objects that fit the serialization or deserialization process.

Using the above approach, in order to implement the findAllItems service, we should create another servlet that does not need to retrieve any input and returns a list of items:

Listing 6—findAllItems Service Implementation

```
protected void doPost(HttpServletRequest request,
                    HttpServletResponse response)
                    throws ServletException, IOException
{
  try {
    JAXBContext jaxbContext = JAXBContext.newInstance
                            (ItemList.class, Item.class);
    ItemList itemList = new ItemList();
    itemList.setList(new ArrayList());

    Item i1 = new Item();
    i1.set ... ;
    itemList.getList().add(i1);

       ... populate itemList ...

      Marshaller marshaller = jaxbContext.createMarshaller();
      marshaller.setProperty(Marshaller.JAXB_FORMATTED_OUTPUT,
                        Boolean.TRUE);
    //Just to see the content of the generated XML message
    marshaller.marshal(itemList, System.out);
```

```
    //Send the XML message to the client
    marshaller.marshal(itemList, response.getOutputStream());
  }
  catch (JAXBException e) {
    throw new ServletException(e);
  }
}
```

Note that we also need to define the ItemList class:

Listing 7—ItemList Binding

```
import java.util.List;
import javax.xml.bind.annotation.XmlRootElement;

@XmlRootElement(name="ItemList")
public class ItemList {
  private List list;
  ...
```

While the correspondent client code may look like this:

Listing 8—findAllItems Service Client Request

```
URL url = new URL("http://localhost/SoaBookPoxHttp/findAllItems");
HttpURLConnection con = (HttpURLConnection) url.openConnection();
con.setRequestMethod("POST");
con.connect();

//Void Request

//Get Response
JAXBContext jaxbContext = JAXBContext.newInstance
                                    (ItemList.class, Item.class);
Unmarshaller unmarshaller = jaxbContext.createUnmarshaller();
ItemList itemList = (ItemList)
                        unmarshaller.unmarshal(con.getInputStream());
for (Iterator iterator = itemList.getList().iterator();
                        iterator.hasNext();)
{
  Item item = (Item) iterator.next();
  System.out.println( item.getId()+" - "+ item.getCode()+" - "+
                        item.getDescription());
}
```

REST—Exploiting the HTTP Protocol

The **Representational State Transfer (REST)** is a web architectural style presented by Roy Fielding back in 2000 in his doctoral thesis. The basic idea of REST is the full exploitation of the HTTP protocol, in particular:

- It focuses on **Resources**, that is, each service should be designed as an action on a resource.

- It takes full advantage of all **HTTP verbs** (not just GET and POST, but also PUT and DELETE).

In the basic POX-over-HTTP example, which we saw previously, you may have noticed that we assumed to use POST as HTTP verb. Although, we listed the source code for just one out of the several services we defined, all of them can be implemented using the same verb (not necessarily POST, any other method will do the job right). Therefore, the idea is, why not exploit this transportation protocol feature to map the usual CRUD and other methods in order to have a clearer communication protocol?

An association between the four CRUD methods and the correspondent HTTP verbs was therefore established and is shown in the following table:

HTTP verb	CRUD action	Action description
POST	CREATE	Save new resources
GET	READ	Read resources
PUT	UPDATE	Modify existing resources
DELETE	DELETE	Delete resources

Keeping in mind that the set of resources, each one with its values, represents the State of the system, the following rules should be applied:

- The State can be modified by verbs POST, PUT, and DELETE.
- The State should never change as a consequence of a GET verb.
- The verb POST should be used to **add** resources to the State.
- The verb PUT should be used to **alter** resources into the State.
- The verb DELETE should be used to **remove** resources from the State.
- The communication protocol should be **stateless**, that is, a call should not depend on the previous ones.

All this may sound quite interesting, but what exactly is a "resource"? Basically, a resource is a scope within which the four HTTP verbs can cover all requested actions. Take for instance the Item domain we explored earlier. Well, that is a good candidate to be treated as a resource. As you see in the implementation source (Listing 5), a switch was introduced (in the if-then block) to do different actions depending on the method name contained in the request. This conditional flow control can be avoided and its role can be done by the HTTP verbs. Let's see how to do that in practice:

In order to create a new Item (the `insertItem` service), an XML document containing the object can be sent to the server with the POST method, while the response may be a generic outcome object:

Listing 9—Outcome Binding

```
@XmlRootElement(name="Outcome")
public class Outcome {
  private String retCode;
  private String retMessaget;
  . . .
}
```

The service code will then be kept small and without the conditional flow instructions for the action to be executed (compare with Listing 5):

Listing 10—REST CREATE Server Implementation

```
protected void doPost(HttpServletRequest request,
                      HttpServletResponse response)
                 throws ServletException, IOException
{
  try{
    JAXBContext jaxbContext = JAXBContext.newInstance
                                (Item.class, Outcome.class);
    Unmarshaller unmarshaller = jaxbContext.createUnmarshaller();
    //Receiving the XML request and transform it into a Java object
    Item item = (Item) unmarshaller.unmarshal
                                (request.getInputStream());
    System.out.println("Inserting item# "+item.getId());
    // ... insert item
    Marshaller marshaller = jaxbContext.createMarshaller();
    marshaller.setProperty(Marshaller.JAXB_FORMATTED_OUTPUT,
                           Boolean.TRUE);
    Outcome outcome = new Outcome();
    outcome.setRetCode("OK");
    outcome.setRetMessaget("Item was inserted successfully");
```

```
    marshaller.marshal(outcome, response.getOutputStream());
  }
  catch (Exception e) {
    throw new ServletException(e);
  }
}
```

Please note that the above is a simple homemade implementation of the REST protocol. We decided to use a basic servlet implementation in order to focus on the key concepts of this communication protocol. However, there are several other ways to adopt REST, for example, by using JAX-WS (which will be used next when exploring SOAP) or with Axis 2.

Coming back to our example, the `updateItem` service can be implemented by analogous source code with the only differences being the servlet method (`doPut` instead of `doPost`) and, of course, the inner update action. Indeed, the REST approach would recommend another difference that we will show a little ahead.

For the insert action, here is an example of the client code:

Listing 11—REST CREATE Client Request

```
Item item = new Item();
item.set...
//Prepare and establish the connection with the service
URL url = new URL("http://localhost/SoaBookREST/itemService");
HttpURLConnection con = (HttpURLConnection) url.openConnection();
con.setDoOutput(true);
//Set the HTTP request method
con.setRequestMethod("POST");
con.connect();
JAXBContext jaxbContext = JAXBContext.newInstance
                                    (Item.class, Outcome.class);
Marshaller marshaller = jaxbContext.createMarshaller();
marshaller.setProperty(Marshaller.JAXB_FORMATTED_OUTPUT,
                  Boolean.TRUE);

//Send the XML request to the service
marshaller.marshal(item, con.getOutputStream());

//Get the XML response from the service and deserialize it
Unmarshaller unmarshaller = jaxbContext.createUnmarshaller();
Outcome outcome = (Outcome)
unmarshaller.unmarshal(con.getInputStream());
```

As far as the `deleteItem`, `findItemById`, and `findAllItems` services are concerned, the REST methodology suggests a slightly different communication protocol. In fact, the above actions do not need to upload an XML document. They just have to pass the object's id or nothing at all (in the `findAllItems` case). In these situations, the called URI, along with the HTTP verb, contains all the information needed to perform the actions. The samples of the REST requests are as shown in the following table:

Verb	URI sample	Action
DELETE	`http://localhost/SoaBookREST/itemService/14`	Delete item #14
GET	`http://localhost/SoaBookREST/itemService/14`	Retrieve item #14
GET	`http://localhost/SoaBookREST/itemService`	Retrieve all items

As you can see, the HTTP request (verb plus URI) tells clearly what is happening, or at least, what is the desired action. Note that now the URI may contain some additional data (the id). So in the web descriptor, we must check to have an URL pattern instead of an exact correspondence:

Listing 12—servlet Mapping Section in web.xml

```
<servlet-mapping>
  <servlet-name>ItemService</servlet-name>
  <url-pattern>/itemService/*</url-pattern>
</servlet-mapping>
```

Here is the service code for the last two actions:

Listing 13—REST READ Service Implementation

```
protected void doGet(HttpServletRequest request,
                     HttpServletResponse response)
                throws ServletException, IOException
{
  try{
    if (request.getPathInfo()==null){
      //findAllItems
      ItemList itemList = new ItemList();
      itemList.setList(new ArrayList());
      //retrieve all items
      ...
      itemList.getList().add(...);
      ...
      //Send the XML message to the client
```

```
        JAXBContext jaxbContext = JAXBContext.newInstance
                                (ItemList.class, Item.class);
        Marshaller marshaller = jaxbContext.createMarshaller();
        marshaller.setProperty(Marshaller.JAXB_FORMATTED_OUTPUT,
                                Boolean.TRUE);
        marshaller.marshal(itemList, response.getOutputStream());
    } else {
      //findItemById
      int id = (new Integer(request.getPathInfo().substring(1)))
            .intValue();
      //retrieve item by id (e.g. from a database)
      Item item = ...
      JAXBContext jaxbContext = JAXBContext.newInstance(Item.class);
      Marshaller marshaller = jaxbContext.createMarshaller();
      marshaller.setProperty(Marshaller.JAXB_FORMATTED_OUTPUT,
                                Boolean.TRUE);
      marshaller.marshal(item, response.getOutputStream());
      }
  }
  catch (Exception e) {
    throw new ServletException(e);
  }
}
```

As far as the **update** action is concerned, the REST style indeed suggests having the object's id in the URI:

```
PUT http://localhost/SoaBookREST/itemService/14
```

In fact, this way, the HTTP request is self-explanatory (it reads "update item #14") in accordance with the REST philosophy.

In general, if you need to create other non-CRUD services with the above technology, the choice falls between:

1. Creating an ad-hoc servlet to be used with an appropriate HTTP verb
2. Re-using an existing servlet and verb with the introduction of some custom logic in the request composition and parsing

Also consider that passing parameters into the request can be a practical alternative to differentiate the control flow, although REST-purists do not like this approach. So, the request could take the form:

```
http://localhost/SoaBookREST/itemService?id=14
```

REST purists may have a point here. In fact, this way we are introducing a dependency on the parameter name (id), and somehow adding complexity to a simple and linear style.

SOAP

The **Simple Object Access Protocol (SOAP)** is a web service standard communication protocol defined by the W3C. It basically defines the structure of the exchanged message, which is composed of an "envelope" with a "header" and a "body". As you will see next, this protocol adds various levels of complexity. But it also offers a wide range of powerful features, among which are:

- Automatic generation of classes involved in the communication process
- Automatic generation of the web service descriptor (WSDL)
- Automatic generation of client classes starting from the service WSDL
- Ability to be used with network protocols other than HTTP (for example, SMTP or JMS)
- Ability to encapsulate authentication mechanisms
- Ability to establish a stateful conversation

In order to show you a straightforward implementation of the services of our domain sample, we will use the JDK 6 embedded capabilities to define and publish web services. In fact, while in the previous examples we exploited the JAXB component to perform the automatic binding between XML documents and Java objects, here we will make use of the JAX-WS library, which will increase the abstraction level significantly.

Look how easy it is to create a couple of services such as insert and update:

Listing 14—JAX-WS Annotations

```
package com.packt.soajava.soap.service.item;

import javax.jws.WebMethod;
import javax.jws.WebService;
import javax.xml.ws.Endpoint;
import com.packt.soajava.model.item.Item;
import com.packt.soajava.model.item.Outcome;

@WebService
public class ItemWs {

  @WebMethod
  public Outcome insert(Item item) {
    //Insert item ...
    System.out.println("Inserting item "+item.getId());
```

```
      Outcome outcome = new Outcome();
      outcome.setRetCode("OK");
      outcome.setRetMessage("Item was inserted successfully");
      return outcome;
  }
  @WebMethod
  public Outcome update(Item item) {
      //Update item ...
      System.out.println("Updating item "+item.getId());
      Outcome outcome = new Outcome();
      outcome.setRetCode("OK");
      outcome.setRetMessage("Item was updated successfully");
      return outcome;
  }
```

As you see the abstraction level here allows a compact and neat source code, without any part dealing with the serialization/deserialization process, just the essential service code. The structure of a web service implemented with SOAP is quite different from what we have seen with the other approaches so far. In fact with basic POX-over-HTTP, we had to create several classes (servlets) for a single functional domain (for example, Item domain), while using REST a single class was needed, but only because our designed methods matched well with the four HTTP verbs. With SOAP, we can have as many methods in a web service as we need, and each one is independent from the other in its signature.

Publishing the above service requires some further steps. First of all, we need to generate the classes involved in the communication process. This is performed by the wsgen utility bundled with JDK 6. Just open a command shell, and run the following line:

```
<JDK6_HOME>\bin\wsgen -cp <ProjectClassesRoot> -d <ProjectSourceRoot>
-keep com.packt.soajava.soap.service.item.ItemWs
```

The above command will generate the needed classes into the <ProjectSourceRoot> (-d=destination directory) folder, given the specified full-path ItemWs class and the classpath (-cp). Now, you should find a new package in the project sources (com.packt.soajava.soap.service.item.**jaxws**), and inside it, there should be four classes. In fact, for each defined web method, two classes will be generated: one with the same name of the method (capitalized) and the other with the same name concatenated with "Response".

The web service is now ready to be published. The JDK 6 makes available, mainly for prototyping usage, a very easy way to do this. Just write and run a class that executes the following line:

```
Endpoint.publish( "http://localhost:8001/SoaBookSOAP_server/itemWs",
                 new ItemWs());
```

We have just published our web service at the specified URI. You may of course change this URI in order to change the URL pattern or port.

How can we check if the service was published correctly? Point your browser to the correspondent WSDL:

```
http://localhost:8001/SoaBookSOAP_server/itemWs?WSDL
```

What you are looking at is the automatically generated **WSDL (Web Service Definition Language)**. Its content represents the structure of the service, and it plays a key role when it comes to have the client classes automatically generated.

The latter action can, in fact, be performed by the wsimport utility:

```
<JDK6_HOME>\bin\wsimport -d <ClientProjectSourceRoot>
   -p com.packt.soajava.soap.client.test.item
   -keep http://localhost:8001/SoaBookSOAP_server/itemWs?WSDL
```

With this command the needed classes will be created into the specified client source folder (-d), using the given package name (-p), and retrieving the service structure at the given URI. Among these classes we will find ItemWsService, the client factory of the web service and ItemWs, an interface supported by the service proxy created by the ItemWsService factory.

Now the client code can be as simple as this:

Listing 15—JAX-WS Sample Client

```
ItemWsService service = new ItemWsService();
ItemWs itemWs = service.getItemWsPort();
Item item1 = new Item();
item1.set ...
Outcome outcome = itemWs.insert(item1);
```

Note that any technology that supports SOAP can generate its own client classes with an automatic process, starting from the published web service descriptor (WSDL).

In the end, with the SOAP approach, we can keep a simple and neat code at both ends of the communication process (the web service implementation and the end client), while the hard work is done by the intermediate auto-generated classes.

RPC and Document Based-WS: How to Communicate, Pros and Cons of the Two Approach

We have just seen how SOAP can leverage the developer's work by doing the entire hard job behind the scenes. Indeed, we have not even seen the content of the XML documents that client and server are exchanging. Well, this can be done using a TCP/IP monitor utility (for example, Apache TCPMon).

Monitoring the request content of the client call, shown in listing 15, gives the following results:

Listing 16—SOAP XML Request

```
<?xml version="1.0" ?>
<soapenv:Envelope
    xmlns:soapenv="http://schemas.xmlsoap.org/soap/envelope/"
    xmlns:xsd="http://www.w3.org/2001/XMLSchema"
    xmlns:ns1="http://item.service.soap.soajava.packt.com/">
  <soapenv:Body>
    <ns1:insert>
    <arg0>
      <code>XY</code>
      <description>xy desc</description>
      <id>26</id>
    </arg0>
    </ns1:insert>
  </soapenv:Body>
</soapenv:Envelope>
```

while the response content is as follows:

Listing 17—SOAP XML Response

```
<?xml version="1.0" ?>
<S:Envelope xmlns:S="http://schemas.xmlsoap.org/soap/envelope/">
  <S:Body>
    <ns2:insertResponse
      xmlns:ns2="http://item.service.soap.soajava.packt.com/">
      <return>
        <retCode>OK</retCode>
        <retMessage>Item was inserted successfully</retMessage>
      </return>
    </ns2:insertResponse>
  </S:Body>
</S:Envelope>
```

As you can see, the XML content of a SOAP message is structured as an `envelope` which contains a mandatory `body`, while the `header` is optional. The content of the body element represents the `payload` that is the exchanged XML document.

However, when dealing with SOAP, a wide range of options are available. In our last example, we just adopted the default settings to keep things simpler and straightforward.

You may have heard, for example, about **binding style** (RCP or Document) or **use** (Encoded or Literal) or **parameter style** (Bare or Wrapped). In this paragraph, we will explore these concepts with particular emphasis on the binding style.

Before getting into this analysis though, we should spend some time on **WS-I**. The term stands for **Web Service — Interoperability** and represents a set of standards put together in order to allow the process of exchanging data throughout web services in a heterogeneous environment (for example, between Java and .NET). Of all the combinations of binding style, use, and parameter style, only the following are WS-I compliant, and we will concentrate exactly on them:

- RPC / literal
- Document / literal (bare or unwrapped)
- Document / literal wrapped

The "encoded" value for the **use** attribute is prohibited by WS-I. With this value, in fact, the data is serialized following the SOAP encoding described in Section 5 of SOAP 1.1 specification. Validating a SOAP encoded message against a WSDL description is quite a hard work, and since the validation is a fundamental step toward interoperability, only the use "literal" is allowed by WS-I.

RPC / Literal

One of the first architectural choices that has to be made when we decide to develop SOAP web services is whether to use RPC or Document binding style. **Remote Procedure Call (RPC)** is a generic mechanism throughout which is a procedure that resides on a computer (or a virtual machine) can be called by a program running on a different computer (or virtual machine). This paradigm has been around for decades and was implemented by several technologies, among which, the most popular are CORBA, DCOM, and RMI.

Despite the changes in technologies, an RPC call is always characterized by:

- A remote address
- A method (or operation) name

- A sequence of parameters
- A synchronous response

Note that, aside from the first, it shares the same characteristics of a classic local method call.

What does this old RPC paradigm have to do with SOAP and web services? Well, quite a lot indeed. In fact, in the early days of its definition (before being publicly published), SOAP was designed to support only RPC. It was, in a sense, a standardized evolution of the various distributed programming technologies.

With some modification in the annotation of the web service we designed last, we can switch it to RPC style (the JAX-WS default is "Document") and begin to explore this approach.

Listing 18—SOAP RPC Style

```
@WebService
@SOAPBinding(style=SOAPBinding.Style.RPC)
public class ItemWs {

   @WebMethod
   public Outcome insert(@WebParam(name="itemParam") Item item,
                         @WebParam(name="categoryParam") String category)
   {
      //Insert item ...
```

As you can see we have introduced another parameter, the `category`, and our goal now is to insert an item into the specified category. We used the `@WebParam` annotation to give a name to each method argument.

Now, let's publish the service (just run the class with the `Endpoint.publish` line, the `wsgen` utility is not required in this case), import the client classes from the published WSDL with `wsimport` utility, and make a client call:

```
Outcome outcome = itemWs.insert(item1, "A");
```

If we monitor the request XML document, we will see the following structure:

Listing 19—SOAP RPC Request

```
<soapenv:Body>
   <ans:insert xmlns:ans="http:// ... ">
      <itemParam>
         <code>XY</code>
         <description>xy desc</description>
         <id>26</id>
      </itemParam>
```

```
                <categoryParam>A</categoryParam>
            </ans:insert>
        </soapenv:Body>
```

where we can recognize the typical RCP parts, that are the method name and the sequence of parameters.

The correspondent WSDL (that may be seen throughout the TCP monitor or pointing the browser to the URL (`http://localhost:8001/SoaBookSOAP_RPC_server/ itemWs?WSDL`) is listed here:

Listing 20—SOAP RPC WSDL

```
<types>
    <xsd:schema>
        <xsd:import schemaLocation="http://127.0.0.1:8002/
                        SoaBookSOAP_RPC_server/itemWs?xsd=1"
                    namespace="http://item.service.
                    soap.soajava.packt.com/"></xsd:import>
    </xsd:schema>
</types>
<message name="insert">
    <part name="itemParam" type="tns:item"></part>
    <part name="categoryParam" type="xsd:string"></part>
</message>
<message name="insertResponse">
    <part name="return" type="tns:outcome"></part>
</message>
<portType name="ItemWs">
    <operation name="insert" parameterOrder=
                                "itemParam categoryParam">
        <input message="tns:insert"></input>
        <output message="tns:insertResponse"></output>
    </operation>
</portType>
<binding name="ItemWsPortBinding" type="tns:ItemWs">
    <soap:binding style="rpc"
                transport="http://schemas.xmlsoap.org/soap/http">
    </soap:binding>
    <operation name="insert">
        <soap:operation soapAction=""></soap:operation>
        <input>
            <soap:body use="literal" namespace=
                    "http://item.service.soap.soajava.packt.com/">
            </soap:body>
        </input>
```

```
            <output>
               <soap:body use="literal" namespace=
                        "http://item.service.soap.soajava.packt.com/">
               </soap:body>
            </output>
         </operation>
      </binding>
      <service name="ItemWsService">
         <port name="ItemWsPort" binding="tns:ItemWsPortBinding">
            <soap:address location=
                  "http://127.0.0.1:8002/SoaBookSOAP_RPC_server/itemWs">
            </soap:address>
         </port>
      </service>
   </definitions>
```

The schema location (`<xsd:schema>` block) is imported from URL:

```
http://127.0.0.1:8001/SoaBookSOAP_RPC_server/itemWs?xsd=1
```

and its content is the following:

Listing 21—SOAP RPC XSD

```
<?xml version="1.0" encoding="UTF-8"?>
  <xs:schema xmlns:tns="http://item.service.soap.soajava.packt.com/"
xmlns:xs="http://www.w3.org/2001/XMLSchema" targetNamespace="http://
item.service.soap.soajava.packt.com/" version="1.0">
      <xs:element name="Item" type="tns:item"></xs:element>
      <xs:element name="Outcome" type="tns:outcome"></xs:element>
      <xs:complexType name="item">
         <xs:sequence>
            <xs:element name="code" type="xs:string"
                        minOccurs="0"></xs:element>
            <xs:element name="description" type="xs:string"
                           minOccurs="0"></xs:element>
            <xs:element name="id" type="xs:int"></xs:element>
         </xs:sequence>
      </xs:complexType>
      <xs:complexType name="outcome">
         <xs:sequence>
            <xs:element name="retCode" type="xs:string"
                          minOccurs="0"></xs:element>
            <xs:element name="retMessage" type="xs:string"
                             minOccurs="0"></xs:element>
         </xs:sequence>
      </xs:complexType>
  </xs:schema>
```

What should be noted here is that the schema defines only the complex type parameters (Item and Outcome in our case). It does not give any information useful to validate either the other simple parameters, or the rest of the SOAP message. Therefore, a major problem in adopting RPC style is that, the exchanged XML documents cannot be validated against an **XML Schema Definition (XSD)**.

Let's explore the Document style and see if it overcomes this limit.

Document / Literal

This style is also known as Document "bare" or "unwrapped" and we will soon get into the explanation of this term. For the moment the thing to pay attention to is that, using JAX-WS, the default value for the parameter style is "wrapped". Hence, in order to use the Document bare style, we have to set it explicitly.

Listing 22—SOAP Document style

```
@SOAPBinding(style=SOAPBinding.Style.DOCUMENT,
             parameterStyle=SOAPBinding.ParameterStyle.BARE)
public class ItemWs {
  @WebMethod
  public Outcome insert(@WebParam(name="itemParam") Item item,
                 @WebParam(name="categoryParam") String category) {
    . . .
```

Now, if we follow the usual steps in order to call this service from a client (again skipping the wsgen step), we will get an error while importing the client classes from the published WSDL.

```
error: operation "insert": more than one part bound to body
```

This is an error that will indeed help us understand the difference between an RPC and a Document approach. What we should know is that WS-I only allows one child in the body of a SOAP message. But what is the reason of such a specification?

The Document style represents a new and different paradigm: the service input is "a document", not a request of the execution of a method with the correspondent parameter value. This means that a single object should be passed, and this object will be the sole input to the web service. The document will contain the information needed to perform its processing, but there is nothing here like a method name or a sequence of parameters. That is the reason why WS-I only allows one child.

Therefore, in order to perform our task (inserting an item into a category) with a Document, using WS-I compliant approach, we should refactor the service. We should create a new object called, for instance, `ItemInsertRequest`, which *wraps* the needed information (the item and the category). That is the reason of the name of this style (bare or unwrapped): there is no wrapping object around the parts; it must be created explicitly.

Listing 23—Request Wrapper

```
@XmlRootElement(name = "ItemInsertRequest")
public class ItemInsertRequest {
  private Item item;
  private String category;
  . . .
```

and the web service refactorized in order to have just one parameter (the document representing the request):

Listing 24—Web Service Using the Defined Wrapper

```
@WebMethod
public Outcome insert(@WebParam(name="itemInsertRequestParam")
ItemInsertRequest itemInsertRequest) {
  . . .
```

In these conditions we will not get errors while generating the client classes with the `wsimport` utility, and can finally make the refactorized client call:

Listing 25—SOAP Document Client Request

```
ItemInsertRequest req = new ItemInsertRequest();
req.setItem(item1);
req.setCategory("A");
Outcome outcome = itemWs.insert(req);
```

that will be forwarded with the following SOAP body:

Listing 26—SOAP Document XML Request

```
<ns1:itemInsertRequestParam>
    <category>A</category>
    <item>
        <code>XY</code>
        <description>xy desc</description>
        <id>26</id>
    </item>
</ns1:itemInsertRequestParam>
```

Please note that, although the structure is indeed the same as with RPC style (see listing 19), we are now dealing with a *document* instead of a method call while the category and item are no more parameters, but just *attributes* of this document.

What should be noted instead about the WSDL is that, other than having *just one part* inside the input message and having the style set to *document*, the attribute *type* has gone missing and a correspondent *element* attribute has taken its place.

Listing 27—SOAP Document WSDL

```
<message name="insert">
    <part element="tns:itemInsertRequestParam"
            name="itemInsertRequestParam"></part>
</message>
. . .
<binding name="ItemWsPortBinding" type="tns:ItemWs">
    <soap:binding style="document"
```

As far as the XML schema is concerned, it can now be used to validate the entire document:

Listing 28—SOAP Document XSD

```
<xs:element name="Item" type="tns:item"></xs:element>
<xs:element name="ItemInsertRequest"
            type="tns:itemInsertRequest"></xs:element>
<xs:element name="Outcome" type="tns:outcome"></xs:element>
<xs:element nillable="true" name="insertResponse"
            type="tns:outcome"></xs:element>
<xs:element nillable="true" name="itemInsertRequestParam"
            type="tns:itemInsertRequest"></xs:element>
<xs:complexType name="itemInsertRequest">
  <xs:sequence>
    <xs:element name="category" type="xs:string"
            minOccurs="0"></xs:element>
    <xs:element name="item" type="tns:item"
            minOccurs="0"></xs:element>
  </xs:sequence>
</xs:complexType>
<xs:complexType name="item">
  <xs:sequence>
    <xs:element name="code" type="xs:string"
            minOccurs="0"></xs:element>
    <xs:element name="description" type="xs:string"
            minOccurs="0"></xs:element>
    <xs:element name="id" type="xs:int"></xs:element>
  </xs:sequence>
</xs:complexType>
```

The main strength of Document/literal style is therefore the ability to allow the validation of the whole XML document exchange.

With this approach, though, we have lost something the operation name is no more present in the SOAP message. This may be a drawback in some situations, take for instance the case where the message is transmitted over an asynchronous TCP/IP protocol such as SMTP. The process of dispatching the message may be difficult, if not impossible.

Another disadvantage of this style is that, if we are dealing with already developed applications, a certain effort has to be taken into account in order to refactor both the server and the client side code.

Document / Literal Wrapped

This style is the default in JAX-WS, and we have already made use of it in our very first SOAP example (see Listing 14). The following annotation is in fact useless with JAX-WS:

Listing 29—SOAP Document Wrapped Style

```
@SOAPBinding(style=SOAPBinding.Style.DOCUMENT,
    parameterStyle=SOAPBinding.ParameterStyle.WRAPPED)
```

Now, let's go back to the initial structure of the web service (before the refactoring needed by the Document bare style):

Listing 30—SOAP Document Wrapped Web Service

```
@WebMethod
public Outcome insert(@WebParam(name="itemParam") Item item,
                @WebParam(name="categoryParam") String category) {
```

and follow the usual steps in order to make a client call (now the wsgen step is required).

Well, now we will not get any error, even if we have more than one parameter, as in RPC style. What does this style do to adhere to the Document style, without forcing us to refactor our source code? It simply *wraps* (automatically, without our effort) the method name and the parameters into a new object, whose name is the same of the method itself.

In fact, the body of the SOAP message is now in this form:

Listing 31—SOAP Document Wrapped XML Request

```
<ns1:insert>
   <itemParam>
      <code>XY</code>
      <description>xy desc</description>
      <id>26</id>
   </itemParam>
   <categoryParam>A</categoryParam>
</ns1:insert>
```

In conclusion, the Document / literal wrapped style gathers the advantages from both Document and RPC approaches:

- The SOAP message can be validated against an XML schema
- The SOAP body contains only one child, and is thus WS-I compliant
- Multiple parameters are allowed without any refactoring
- The operation name is contained in the message

It is, in fact, the default when we use JAX-WS and in general a good choice for most cases.

Why We Should Use Doc-WS?

The RPC Inheritance

In the previous paragraph, we introduced the difference between RPC and Document style. At first, one can argue that, after all, examining the exchanged messages and their WSDL, the two approaches are not that different, especially the RPC and Document wrapped ones. Well, in a sense, this is true.

The difference is indeed more philosophical than practical, at least for most of us accustomed for decades to the "method call" paradigm. We may have gone through several programming languages and technologies, but we always could count on a rock pillar that is of being able to call a method (sometimes named "procedure", "function", or whatever) passing a sequence of parameters and (optionally) getting the result.

In this scenario, when SOAP was initially conceived, web services were more or less an extension of this model in order to allow the call of a remote procedure (RPC) in a more standardized fashion. In fact, as mentioned before, the initial SOAP specification was based upon RPC style.

The Document-Oriented Way

Now, we intend to show how the Document approach is shifting the focus for a new programming model that will arguably take the leading way in the future.

A document is similar to a message, that is, something to be "sent" or "forwarded" to a destination which is designed to process it.

Document Style

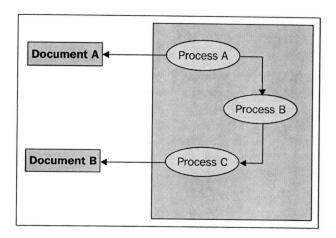

Self-Containing Documents and Asynchronous Models

We should not focus on when this processing will take place, but must instead ensure that the message contains all the information needed for the processing itself. Therefore, the message should be a self-contained business document. This is a fundamental prerequisite when dealing with an asynchronous transportation protocol (for example SMTP or JMS, both supported by SOAP), but is anyway a good practice even when not explicitly required.

Another situation where a self-contained business document is a requirement is when a *work-flow system* is used. In fact, since the transitions inside a work-flow are intrinsically asynchronous, the Document style fits well in this scenario.

Validating Capabilities

We have already highlighted one intrinsic advantage of this style: the capability to perform a full validation of the exchanged documents against their correspondent XML schemas.

Loose Coupling

One of the major weaknesses of the RPC approach is the tight coupling that it imposes on architectures. A change in a service method signature has an immediate impact throughout the system, forcing the refactoring up to the client layer. With Document style, the problem is drastically reduced since a change in the structure of a message (like, adding a new attribute) does not affect the document exchange mechanisms. On the other hand, a change in a back-end (internal) method signature has generally no effect upon the messages structure.

This loose coupling, intrinsic in the Document style, leads to more robust and reliable architectures that are easier to maintain, and having a modular aspect.

Interoperability

Finally, we have to consider the value of interoperability, which is the ability to work together with different technologies and systems. This can be obtained primarily by adhering to standard communication protocols and directives, with an eye open though, to the market trends. The Document style is gaining consensus and is largely adopted by most vendors. It is a matter of fact that both the Java reference implementation of JAX-WS, along with most other Java WS implementations (see Chapter 6), and the .NET platform use the Document style as the default setting.

Implementations: JAX-WS 2, Axis2, Spring-WS, and XFire/CXF 2.0

In the path towards web services, we need to choose, at some point, the implementation that we intend to adopt. The choice may depend upon a number of factors. In this paragraph, we will examine some of the main implementation focusing on their features and peculiarities in order to make the choice easier.

JAX-WS 2

We have indeed already been introduced to JAX-WS in the previous paragraphs. What should be noted first, about this option, is that it is a specification (JSR-224), rather than an implementation. In fact, its name stands for "**Java API for XML Web Services**" and it follows the previous **JAX-RPC (Java API for XML-based Remote Procedure Call)** specification.

One of the main advantages of this choice is that its Reference Implementation is included both into Java SE 6 and Java EE 5. Thus no external library is needed in order to use it. If you adopt this embedded version, then you will be working with the **version 2.0** of the product, though, at the time of writing, it has reached **version 2.1** as a separate implementation.

As far as the data binding model is concerned, it uses JAXB, while the XML parser engine is the stream-based pull parser **StAX (Streaming API for XML)**. This parsing approach, where the client gets XML data only when requested, allows better performances compared to a DOM-based approach, where the entire XML document is parsed to obtain an in-memory object tree. In fact, not only is the requested memory footprint smaller, but also there is the advantage of having the parser start its process earlier.

JAX-WS supports both SOAP and REST communication protocols, though RESTful services cannot take advantage of the automatic code generation (in contrast with the SOAP/WSDL approach) since a standard for RESTful services description has not yet been defined.

It strongly relies on the usage of annotations and supports a number of transportation protocols, going beyond HTTP including SMTP and JMS.

Moreover the range of WS-* features covered is indeed wide. It goes from WS-Security and Policy to WS-Atomic Transaction and WS-ReliableMessaging.

Finally, among its features, there is also the capability to build Stateful web services.

Axis 2

This tool is part of "Web Service Project @ Apache", a set of several projects that cover various aspects related to the development and usage of web services. They are for the majority implementations of protocols and specifications.

Axis2 is a complete re-factoring of the previous **1.x version**, and upon its architecture two different implementations were built, Axis2/Java and Axis2/C.

The SAX event-based XML parser used in the previous version has been replaced by the pull-based StAX, which allows greater control over the document processing that translates into higher efficiency and performances.

Indeed Axis2 uses **AXIOM (AXIs Object Model)**, a light-weight object model for XML processing, which is based on StAX and offers enhancing features.

Axis2 can be used to develop both SOAP-based and RESTful web services. Also, it supports Asynchronous (or Non-Blocking) web services invocation, which is implemented by Callback mechanisms.

It has been designed with a modular and extensible architecture. The processes of sending and receiving the SOAP messages are performed by two "Pipes" (or "Flows"): **the In Pipe and Out Pipe.** Each pipe is designed to process the message throughout a sequence of phases which can have pluggable "Handlers", there by giving the whole architecture a high-level of extensibility. In fact, in addition to built-in phases, there is the option to add User-defined phases with custom handlers inside them, in order to perform new mechanisms or to override existing ones.

Another important level of Handlers grouping is the concept of Module. Each module defines a set of handlers, and a descriptor of the phase rules. A handler can specify not only the phase where it will perform its action, but also its execution order inside the phase throughout the phase rules. In the Axis2 language, a module is "available" when it is present in the system, though not active. The activation of a module turns it to the "engaged" state, after which its handlers are placed into their associated phases and enabled. Thus, it is easy, for example, to plug-in modules that handle WS-* specifications such as WS-Security (Apache Rampart module) or WS-Atomic Transaction (Apache Kandula2 module).

The data binding is not part of the core of Axis2, but it is provided by an extension mechanism that allows the choice among **ABD (Axis Data Binding)**, XMLBeans, JAX-Me, and JibX. Also, the range of the transmission protocols supported is complete (HTTP, TCP, SMTP, and JMS).

The default Axis2 installation procedure consists of deploying the "WAR distribution" to the application server (for Tomcat (the declared recommended container) and just copying the file into the CATALINA_HOME/webapps directory). This will deploy the "axis2" web application (the Axis2 Administration Application) that allows the addition and configuration of services and modules.

Please note that services, modules, phases, and handlers are configured in an independent way with respect to the other deployed web applications. In other words, if you have a set of deployed web applications, each with its own business layer, you will not put a service into one of these web applications. Instead, it will be defined and configured into axis2 application and therefore generally available to every consumer (a client or another server application).

Also consider that every configuration made with the Axis2 Administration Application will not be saved and will therefore be lost after a restart of Axis2 application. Now, the situation will go back to the manually edited configuration files.

Alternatively, you can install the "standard binary distribution", which includes, in addition to all the necessary jars, a number of command line tools for:

- Generating the Java code from the WSDL file, and vice versa (java2wsdl and wsdl2java).

- Starting a simple standalone server (axis2server), where you can deploy your services.

- Starting a java application with the automatic loading of the entire needed library (axis2).

Spring-WS

Spring Framework is certainly one of the more popular and interesting products today available in the Java development area. It has definitely revolutionized the approach to designing software projects. With its aspect-oriented philosophy, and the introduction of the concept of "Inversion of Control (IoC)" or "Dependency Injection", it has made the process of building the architecture of a J2EE application easier and cleaner. But Spring is much more than an IoC container. It provides out-of-the-box patterns and templates, and integrates well with a number of other frameworks and tools, brings flexibility, modularity, and robustness.

This great community has made, among the others, its contribution to the web services area, and its name is "Spring Web Services" or "Spring-WS".

Therefore, an immediate advantage in adopting this framework is the inheritance of the Spring concepts and patterns, as well as, the re-use of the know-how you may have already consolidated. The loose coupling between the service contract (or interface) and its implementation is, for example, one of the first pros of this choice.

A mainstream web service recipe recommends starting the designing from the WSDL (contract-first) rather than from the Java code. Spring-WS pushes this approach further, driving the designer to start from the schemas (XSD) of the input and output XML messages. The WSDL will then be automatically generated from the XSDs.

The XML handling can be configured to use a DOM-based library (W3C DOM, JDOM, dom4j, XOM), SAX, StAX and XPath, while for XML binding, you can choose between JAXB, Castor, XMLBeans, JiBX, and XStream.

Spring-WS has a powerful and flexible Message Dispatcher which can handle the XML message distribution.

Particular care has been dedicated to the WS-Security aspects regarding Authentication, Digital signatures, Encryption, and Decryption.

XFire / CXF

XFire has been developed with the goal of obtaining better performance with respect to Axis 1.x (the de facto standard at that time). In fact, it uses a fast object model based on StAX.

It is simple and easy to use; it provides support for several binding libraries: JAXB, Castor, and XMLBeans. But the default is Aegis Binding—a fast binding mechanism with a small memory requirement.

XFire integrates well with many containers, among which are Spring and PicoContainer (another Inversion-of-Control framework). A set of easy-to-use client API makes it easy to build the client side, and to develop unit tests. The transports supported are HTTP, JMS, and Jabber/XMPP.

Recently, XFire and another web service framework, Celtix, have converged to a new product, CXF 2.0, which should be considered the continuation of XFire 1.x. The goal of this new tool is to go further in the directions of high performances, and ease of use.

CXF supports a number of protocols in addition to SOAP, including REST (via Annotations) and CORBA. It adheres to several standards and WS-* specifications.

Its focus is also on being made embeddable into other programs and pushes on the code-first methodology instead of contract-first.

Summary

In this chapter, we examined the relationship between the SOA methodology and the basics of web service implementation. We saw how XML can be used as the common language to decouple the communication between web services implementations and their consumer clients. From a basic XML-over-HTTP approach to the REST and SOAP protocols, we got into the details of how web services can be implemented with various degrees of complexity and flexibility. Further, while exploring the options of the SOAP protocol, we dissected the difference between adopting an RPC or a Document style. In particular, the Document style showed its advantages over RPC. In fact, it is largely adopted as the default style by the majority of the web service implementation frameworks.

3
Web Service Implementations

In Chapter 2, we looked into samples demonstrating basic SOA with POX over HTTP and we have also seen an introduction to SOAP. Today SOAP is so indispensible a technology, and standard, as most of the B2B communications across trading partners happen over this. Whether SOAP, as its name implies, is simple or not is still disputed. However, one aspect which everyone agrees with is its open standards-based nature and the industry wide support available in the form of tools and frameworks. Almost all web services stacks adopts SOAP as the de-facto over the wire protocol. This is true with many Java web services framework too. Now, to implement your own web services in Java, or to access a third-party web service from within your Java code, you need to understand the various options existing today so that you can make decisions. This chapter is intended to introduce major web service implementations available in the Java/J2EE world. So, we will cover the following in this chapter:

- WS using JAX-WS 2.0
- WS using Apache Axis
- WS using Spring
- WS using XFire

We will have code samples and build files starting from scratch demonstrating how to set up web services and how to access an existing web service using the above web service implementations.

Web Service Using JAX-WS 2.0

JAX-WS stands for **Java API for XML Web Services**. The JAX-WS 2.0 specification replaces JAX-RPC 1.0 and is the next generation web services API-based on JSR 224.

JAX-WS 2.0—A Primer

The JAX-WS 2.0 project develops and evolves the code base for the reference implementation of the JAX-WS specification and is available in the URL `https://jax-ws.dev.java.net/`. At present the code base supports JAX-WS 2.0 and JAXWS 2.1.

The following list specifies new features implemented by JAX-WS 2.0:

- Direct support for JAXB 2.0-based data binding
- Support for the latest W3C and WS-I standards (e.g. SOAP 1.2, WSDL 1.2, and SAAJ 1.3)
- Standardized metadata for Java to WSDL (and vice versa) mapping
- Ease-of-development features
- Support for easier evolution of web services
- Improved handler framework
- Support for asynchronous RPC and non-HTTP transports

Another exciting feature of JAX-WS 2.0 is the support it has got within Java Platform, Standard Edition 6 (Java SE 6). This means, JAX-WS 2.0-based code and components can be executed from within a fully blown J2EE server infrastructure such as Project GlassFish, or with just Java SE 6. This is indeed a great advantage for Java developers, which has been previously enjoyed only by .NET developers (.NET stack supports web services development in the light-weight manner).

JAX-WS 2.0 provides the following new APIs in the Java SE 6 platform to build web applications and web services:

API	Package
JAX-WS	javax.xml.ws
SAAJ	javax.xml.soap
WS Metadata	javax.jws

Web Service Implementation in Java SE 6

First things first and simple things foremost! In this section, you will not use any application server or any third-party web server, but will use just Java SE 6 and its tools to develop and deploy a simple web service.

Code Server and Client

As said earlier, we will start with our simple samples first. The code artifacts for our first sample are placed in the folder ch03\01_JaxWS\JavaStandAlone.

The server is composed of three Java files kept in folder ch03\01_JaxWS\ JavaStandAlone\Server\src and are explained below:

IHello.java

IHello is a java interface and is shown here:

```
public interface IHello{
    String sayHello (String name);
}
```

HelloImpl.java

HelloImpl implements the business functionality to be exposed as web service. This class realizes the preceding IHello interface:

```
import javax.jws.WebService;
import javax.jws.soap.SOAPBinding;
import javax.jws.WebMethod;
@WebService(name="IHello", serviceName="HelloService")
@SOAPBinding(style=SOAPBinding.Style.RPC)
public class HelloImpl implements IHello{
    @WebMethod(operationName = "sayHello")
    public String sayHello(String name){
        System.out.println("HelloImpl.sayHello...");
        return "\nHello From Server !! : " + name;
    }
}
```

HelloImpl is annoted with javax.jws.WebService annotation. The @WebService annotation defines the class as a web service endpoint. The javax.jws.soap. SOAPBinding annotation specifies the mapping of the web service onto the SOAP message protocol. HelloImpl declares a single method named sayHello, which is annotated with the @WebMethod annotation. This annotation will expose the annotated method to web service clients. In fact, the IHello interface is not required while building a JAX-WS endpoint, but we have used it here as a good programming practice.

HelloServer.java

`HelloServer` is a main class which makes use of `javax.xml.ws.Endpoint` for publishing the web service:

```
import javax.xml.ws.Endpoint;
public class HelloServer {
    public static void main(String args[]) {
        log("HelloServer.main : Creating HelloImpl...");
        IHello iHello = new HelloImpl();
        try{
            // Create and publish the endpoint at the given address
            log("HelloServer.main : Publishing HelloImpl...");
            Endpoint endpoint1 =
                Endpoint.publish("http://localhost:8080/Hello", iHello);
            log("HelloServer.main : Published Implementor...");
        }
        catch (Exception e) {
            System.err.println("ERROR: " + e);
            e.printStackTrace(System.out);
        }
        System.out.println("HelloServer Exiting ...");
    }
}
```

HelloClient.java

The Client is composed of one Java file kept in folder `ch03\01_JaxWS\ JavaStandAlone\Client\src`. The `HelloClient` is dependent on two auto generated classes for example, `HelloService` and `IHello`. These classes will be auto generated, when we will build the client later in this exercise. The following code of client is straightforward:

```
public class HelloClient{
    public static void main(String args[]) {
        log("HelloClient.main : Creating HelloImpl...");
        HelloService helloService = null;
        IHello helloImpl = null;
        String gotFromServer = null;
        try{
            log("HelloClient.main : Creating HelloImplService...");
            if(args.length != 0){
                helloService = new HelloService(new URL(args[0]),
                    new QName(args[1], args[2]));
            }
            else{
                helloService = new HelloService();
            }
            log("HelloClient.main : Retreiving HelloImpl...");
```

```
        helloImpl = helloService.getIHelloPort();
        log("HelloClient.main : Invoking
            helloImpl.sayHello(\"Binil\")...");
        gotFromServer = helloImpl.sayHello("Binil");
        log("HelloClient.main : gotFromServer : " + gotFromServer);
    }
    catch (Exception e) {
        System.err.println("ERROR: " + e);
        e.printStackTrace(System.out);
    }
  }
}
```

You will first have to instantiate the `HelloService`, which has the required plumping to connect to the web service. Then, you will get a reference to the port using which you can invoke the remote web service.

Run the Server and Client

As a first step and if you haven't done it before, edit examples.`PROPERTIES` provided along with the code download for this chapter and change the paths there to match your development environment. The code download for this chapter also includes a `README.txt` file, which gives detailed steps to build and run the samples.

To build the server and bring up the server in a single command, it is easy for you to go to ch03\`01_JaxWS\JavaStandAlone` folder and execute the following command:

```
cd ch03\01_JaxWS\JavaStandAlone
ant server
```

Once the server is up and running, you can execute `ant client` command in a different prompt.

When we build the client, we also auto generate some client side artifacts out of the deployed web service using the following ant task:

```
<target name="GenSrc">
    <exec executable="${env.JAVA_HOME}/bin/wsimport">
        <arg line="-keep
                    -d build
                    -p com.binildas.ws.javastandalone.simple
                    -s ${gensrc}  http://localhost:8080/Hello?WSDL"/>
    </exec>
</target>
```

The client code is dependent on these generated files. So, we can now build the client codebase, and then send a web service request to the server. Any response received from the server is printed to the console. The following commands build and run the client in a single go.

```
cd ch03\01_JaxWS\JavaStandAlone
ant client
```

```
Command Prompt                                        _ □ ×

D:\binil\com\java\com\binildas\mytextbooks\soaandjava\3216_0
3_Code\ch03\01_JaxWS\JavaStandAlone>ant client
Buildfile: build.xml

client:

clean:

init:
    [mkdir] Created dir: D:\binil\com\java\com\binildas\myte
xtbooks\soaandjava\3216_03_Code\ch03\01_JaxWS\JavaStandAlone
\Client\build
    [mkdir] Created dir: D:\binil\com\java\com\binildas\myte
xtbooks\soaandjava\3216_03_Code\ch03\01_JaxWS\JavaStandAlone
\Client\gensrc

GenSrc:
    [exec] parsing WSDL...
    [exec]
    [exec]
    [exec] generating code...

compileStub:

compileClient:
    [javac] Compiling 1 source file to D:\binil\com\java\com
\binildas\mytextbooks\soaandjava\3216_03_Code\ch03\01_JaxWS\
JavaStandAlone\Client\build

all:

run:
    [echo] Running example client
    [java] HelloClient.main : Creating HelloImpl...
    [java] HelloClient.main : Creating HelloImplService...
    [java] HelloClient.main : Retreiving HelloImpl...
    [java] HelloClient.main : Invoking helloImpl.sayHello("
Binil")...
    [java] HelloClient.main : gotFromServer :
    [java] Hello From Server !! : Binil

BUILD SUCCESSFUL
Total time: 5 seconds
D:\binil\com\java\com\binildas\mytextbooks\soaandjava\3216_0
3_Code\ch03\01_JaxWS\JavaStandAlone>
```

Web Service Implementation in Java EE Server

Let us now move on to an Enterprise Server and deploy a similar web service there. For running the samples in this section, we will go with the Java EE 5 SDK Update 4 for Windows (`java_ee_sdk-5_04-windows-nojdk.exe`), which is available for download at `http://java.sun.com/javaee/downloads/index.jsp`.

Install and Start the Server

If you already have the latest version of JDK installed in your machine, you may choose to download the 'nojdk' version of the installable, or else you need to download the 'Java EE + JDK' version. Double-click and install the Java EE Server into some location in your hard drive (preferably to a file path with no spaces and fancy characters).

To start the default domain of the Java EE Server, it is easy for you to select the **Start Default Server** option from the **Programs** menu:

```
Start -> All Programs -> Sun Microsystems -> Java EE 5 SDK -> Start
Default Server
```

Now, you can verify whether your server is up by typing:

`http://127.0.0.1:8080/`

You will be able to see the Sun Java System Application Server 9.1_01 (build b09d-fcs) welcome page.

You can also bring up the admin console by typing the following URL:

`http://localhost:4848`

Sometimes, you will also find it easy to start your server by going to the following path and typing the following command:

```
cd %J2EE_HOME%\lib
asadmin-pause start-domain domain1
```

Here, J2EE_HOME points to the root folder where you have deployed your Java EE Server.

```
D:\Applns\Java\java_ee_sdk-5_04\lib>asadmin-pause start-doma
in domain1
Starting Domain domain1, please wait.
Log redirected to D:\Applns\Java\java_ee_sdk-5_04\domains\do
main1\logs\server.log.
Redirecting output to D:/Applns/Java/java_ee_sdk-5_04/domain
s/domain1/logs/server.log
Domain domain1 is ready to receive client requests. Addition
al services are being started in background.
Domain [domain1] is running [Sun Java System Application Ser
ver 9.1_01 (build b09d-fcs)] with its configuration and logs
 at: [D:\Applns\Java\java_ee_sdk-5_04\domains].
Admin Console is available at [http://localhost:4848].
Use the same port [4848] for "asadmin" commands.
User web applications are available at these URLs:
[http://localhost:8080 https://localhost:8181 ].
Following web-contexts are available:
[/web1  /__wstx-services Hello ].
Standard JMX Clients (like JConsole) can connect to JMXServi
ceURL:
[service:jmx:rmi:///jndi/rmi://TUMKVML26327:8686/jmxrmi] for
 domain management purposes.
Domain listens on at least following ports for connections:
[8080 8181 4848 3700 3820 3920 8686 ].
Domain does not support application server clusters and othe
r standalone instances.

Press any key to continue . . .

D:\Applns\Java\java_ee_sdk-5_04\lib>asadmin-pause stop-domai
n domain1
Domain domain1 stopped.
Press any key to continue . . .

D:\Applns\Java\java_ee_sdk-5_04\lib>_
```

Code Server and Client

The server and client files are kept in the folder ch03\01_JaxWS\JavaEEServer\src and are explained here:

HelloWebService.java

HelloWebService is again an annotated java class. The annotations have the same meaning as in the earlier sample.

```
@WebService
public class HelloWebService{
    private static int times;
    public HelloWebService(){
        System.out.println("Inside HelloWebService.HelloWebService...");
```

```
    }
    public String hello(String param){
        System.out.println("Inside HelloWebService.hello... - " +
            (++times));
        return "Return From Server : Hello " + param;
    }
}
```

Client.java

The code for the client is very simple and is shown here:

```
public class Client{
@WebServiceRef(wsdlLocation = "http://localhost:8080/
    HelloWebService/HelloWebServiceService?WSDL")
    static HelloWebServiceService service;
    public static void main(String[] args){
        Client client = new Client();
        client.test();
    }
    public void test(){
        try{
            HelloWebService helloWebServicePort =
                service.getHelloWebServicePort();
            String ret =
                helloWebServicePort.hello(System.getProperty(
                                          "user.name"));
            System.out.println("Hello result = " + ret);
        }
        catch(Exception e){
            e.printStackTrace();
        }
    }
}
```

Here, we use the `javax.xml.ws.WebServiceRef` annotation to declare a reference to the deployed web service. `@WebServiceRef` uses the `wsdlLocation` element to specify the URI of the `HelloWebService`'s WSDL file. Then, the client gets a proxy to the remote web service and invokes the web service method.

Run the Server and Client

Again, to keep things simple, we will not do standard packaging in this sample. Instead, compile the web service class directly into the `autodeploy` directory of the Java EE Server, `%J2EE_HOME%\ domains\domain1\autodeploy`.

We can do the following steps in a single ant command:

- Build the Server and Client
- Deploy the Server into default domain
- Run the client to send web service request to the server

For this, assuming your Java EE server is up and running, execute the following command:

```
cd ch03\01_JaxWS\JavaEEServer
ant
```

The following figure shows what you can see in the console. Here, the client first sends a request to the server and any response returned by the server is then printed out in the client side console.

```
Command Prompt                                           _ □ ×
D:\binil\com\java\com\binildas\mytextbooks\soaandjava\3216_0
3_Code\ch03\01_JaxWS\JavaEEServer>ant
Buildfile: build.xml

init:

clean:
    [delete] Deleting directory D:\binil\com\java\com\binilda
s\mytextbooks\soaandjava\3216_03_Code\ch03\01_JaxWS\JavaEESe
rver\build

compile-deploy-service:
    [mkdir] Created dir: D:\binil\com\java\com\binildas\myte
xtbooks\soaandjava\3216_03_Code\ch03\01_JaxWS\JavaEEServer\b
uild
    [echo] D:/Applns/Java/java_ee_sdk-5_04
    [javac] Compiling 1 source file to D:\Applns\Java\java_e
e_sdk-5_04\domains\domain1\autodeploy

get-artifacts-windows:
    [exec] parsing WSDL...
    [exec]
    [exec]
    [exec] generating code...
    [exec]
    [exec]
    [exec] compiling code...
    [exec]

get-artifacts-unix:

get-artifacts:

compile-client:
    [javac] Compiling 1 source file to D:\binil\com\java\com
\binildas\mytextbooks\soaandjava\3216_03_Code\ch03\01_JaxWS\
JavaEEServer\build

run-client-windows:
    [exec] Hello result = Return From Server : Hello Binil_
Christudas

run-client-unix:

run-client:

all:

BUILD SUCCESSFUL
Total time: 11 seconds
D:\binil\com\java\com\binildas\mytextbooks\soaandjava\3216_0
3_Code\ch03\01_JaxWS\JavaEEServer>
```

The WSDL for the deployed web service would be available in the URL
`http://localhost:8080/HelloWebService/HelloWebServiceService?WSDL`

Web Service Using Apache Axis

Apache Axis is an implementation of the SOAP ("Simple Object Access Protocol") submission to W3C. Axis is a reliable and stable base to implement Java Web services, and there are many companies who use Axis for web services support in their products. Moreover, there is a very active user community too for Axis. Axis comes in two forms. for example, Axis 1.x and Axis 2. Axis 2 architecture is recent as compared to the predecessor, and is a redesign of Axis 1.x supporting SOAP 1.2, SOAP1.2, REST and more. There are many production deployments in 1.x code base too. For our discussion, we will use Axis 1.3, which you can download from the URL `http://ws.apache.org/axis/java/releases.html`.

Contract-First versus Contract-Last

There are two approaches commonly adopted for defining and implementing web services, Contract-first and Contract-last. In the Contract-first approach, we start with a web service contract, which is a WSDL file. We use tools to generate java artifacts out of the WSDL file. These generated artifacts includes java interfaces and implementation classes as well as any other web services plumbing related code. Whereas in the Contract-last approach, you start with the Java code, and let the WSDL be generated from that.

Even though, the approach to be adopted depends on many factors including the context in which you are defining your web services, the Contract-first approach is preferred in normal circumstances. But one practical difficulty in the Contract-first approach is that creating a WSDL is not a trivial process and hence we may not be able to do that easily without some special tool support. To deal with this difficulty, there is a mixed approach which we can follow, whose steps are as follows:

- Create the web service interface (Java interface) alone first
- Generate WSDL out of this interface
- Now follow the normal steps which you follow in the Contract-first approach

We will follow this mixed approach in our samples. Hence, you will be able to adopt the samples here to follow either the Contract-first or the Contract-last approach by doing simple changes to the build scripts.

Web Service Implementation in Axis

We will use Axis 1.3, which is freely downloadable from the URL
`http://ws.apache.org/axis/java/releases.html`. Unzip the installation to a
suitable location in your hard drive and change the `axis.home` path in `examples.`
`PROPERTIES` to point to this location.

Different from the previous samples in this chapter, we will now build and package
the web services files as a standard web archive (`.war`). We would then require a
web server to deploy the web archive. We will use Apache Tomcat 6.x, which you
can again download freely from the URL `http://tomcat.apache.org/`.

Code Server and Client

We will implement the server in a Contract-first approach, but since we don't want
to hand code the WSDL, let's start with a Java interface. All the required files for this
sample are placed in the folder `ch03\02_Axis\src`. Let's look into these files one
by one.

IHelloWeb.java

`IHelloWeb` is a simple Java interface, which defines a business method as
shown here:

```
public interface IHelloWeb{
    public String hello(String param);
}
```

In the Contract-first approach, we start from a WSDL. As WSDL is language and
platform neutral, we are sure that the client and server implemented in the Contract-
first approach will be able to interoperate. But in our sample, we can start with a
Java interface and then generate WSDL. So, in order to make sure that this generated
WSDL is also compliant to interoperable standards, you need to pay attention to
the parameters and return types of the method declaration in the java interface.
Before you generate the WSDL make sure that the types in this Java interface can be
interpreted as standard, portable types in the WSDL too.

HelloWebService.java

Now we need to implement the web service. `HelloWebService` class will just do that.

```
public class HelloWebService implements IHelloWeb{
    private static int times;
    public HelloWebService(){
        System.out.println("Inside HelloWebService.HelloWebService...");
```

```
    }
    public String hello(String param){
        System.out.println("Inside HelloWebService.hello... - " +
            (++times));
        return "Return From Server";
    }
}
```

Now, instead of creating the web service implementation class from scratch, we can generate an implementation template class. Into this template, you can manually add your business logic. OK, that is the method for your production deployments, but for this sample, you don't need to do these manual steps. Instead, we will try to do everything automatic using a smart ant build file.

build.xml

The `build.xml` file is important, since it takes you step by step, starting from a Java interface through implementing business logic, and then packaging as a standard web archive. So, we will reproduce the entire build file here.

```xml
<?xml version="1.0" ?>
<project default="all">

    <property file="../examples.properties"/>
    <property name="build" value="build"/>
    <property name="dist" value="dist"/>
    <property name="lib" value="lib"/>
    <property name="src" value="src"/>
    <property name="gensrc" value="gensrc"/>
    <property name="config" value="config"/>
    <property name="webapp.name" value="AxisEndToEnd"/>
    <property name="service.name" value="HelloWebService"/>
    <property name="wsdl" value="HelloWebService.wsdl"/>
    <property name="interface.package"
        value="com.binildas.apache.axis.AxisEndToEnd"/>
    <property name="interface.path"
        value="com/binildas/apache/axis/AxisEndToEnd"/>
    <property name="interface.class" value="IHelloWeb"/>
    <property name="implement.package"
        value="com.binildas.apache.axis.AxisEndToEnd"/>
    <property name="implement.path"
        value="com/binildas/apache/axis/AxisEndToEnd"/>
    <property name="implement.class" value="HelloWebService"/>
    <path id="classpath">
        <pathelement path="./build"/>
```

```
        <fileset dir="${axis.home}/lib">
            <include name="*.jar"/>
        </fileset>
    </path>
    <target name="all" depends=" deploy, compileclient">
    </target>
    <target name="clean">
        <delete dir="${build}"/>
        <delete dir="${dist}"/>
        <delete dir="${lib}"/>
        <delete dir="${gensrc}"/>
    </target>
    <target name="init">
        <mkdir dir="${build}"/>
        <mkdir dir="${dist}"/>
        <mkdir dir="${lib}"/>
        <mkdir dir="${gensrc}"/>
    </target>
    <target name="copy">
        <copy todir="${lib}">
            <fileset dir="${axis.home}/lib">
                <include name="*.jar"/>
            </fileset>
        </copy>
    </target>
    <target name="precompile" depends="clean, init">
        <javac srcdir="${src}" destdir="build" classpathref="classpath">
            <exclude name="**/*Client*.java"/>
        </javac>
    </target>
    <target name="java2wsdl" depends="precompile">
        <java classname="org.apache.axis.wsdl.Java2WSDL" fork="true"
            failonerror="true">
            <arg value="-o"/>
            <arg value="${wsdl}"/>
            <arg value="-lhttp://localhost:8080/${webapp.name}/
                services/${service.name}"/>
            <arg value="${interface.package}.${interface.class}"/>
            <classpath>
                <path refid="classpath"/>
                <pathelement location="${build}"/>
            </classpath>
        </java>
```

```
    </target>
    <target name="wsdl2java" depends="java2wsdl">
        <java classname="org.apache.axis.wsdl.WSDL2Java" fork="true"
              failonerror="true">
            <arg value="-o"/>
            <arg value="${gensrc}"/>
            <arg value="-s"/>
            <arg value="-S"/>
            <arg value="no"/>
            <arg value="-c"/>
            <arg value="${implement.package}.${implement.class}"/>
            <arg value="${wsdl}"/>
            <classpath>
                <path refid="classpath"/>
                <pathelement location="${build}"/>
            </classpath>
        </java>
    </target>
    <target name="implement" depends="wsdl2java">
        <delete>
            <fileset dir="${gensrc}/${implement.path}"
                includes="${implement.class}.java"/>
        </delete>
        <copy todir="${gensrc}/${implement.path}" overwrite="ture">
            <fileset dir="${src}/${implement.path}">
                <include name="${implement.class}.java"/>
            </fileset>
        </copy>
    </target>
    <target name="compile" depends="implement">
        <javac srcdir="${gensrc}" destdir="build"
            classpathref="classpath"/>
    </target>
    <target name="compileclient">
        <javac srcdir="${src}" destdir="build" classpathref="classpath">
            <include name="**/*Client*.java"/>
        </javac>
    </target>
    <target name="deploy" depends="compile, copy">
        <move todir="${config}" flatten="yes">
            <fileset dir="${gensrc}">
                <include name="**/*.wsdd"/>
```

```
            </fileset>
        </move>
        <java classname="org.apache.axis.utils.Admin" fork="true"
              failonerror="true" dir="config">
            <arg value="server"/>
            <arg file="config/deploy.wsdd" />
            <classpath>
                <path refid="classpath"/>
                <pathelement location="build"/>
            </classpath>
        </java>
        <war destfile="dist/${webapp.name}.war" webxml="config/web.xml">
            <webinf dir="config">
                <include name="server-config.wsdd"/>
            </webinf>
            <lib dir="lib"/>
            <classes dir="build"/>
        </war>
        <delete dir="${lib}"/>
    </target>
</project>
```

Let us now understand the implementation of the web service step by step. We will execute the following ant targets, in the same order.

- `clean`: This will delete all temporary folders and any generated files in the previous build.

- `init`: This will create a few, new folders.

- `precompile`: In this step, the aim is to compile the interface class.

- `java2wsdl`: The `java2wsdl` will generate the WSDL from the precompiled java interface. You can look at the URL http://ws.apache.org/axis/java/reference.html to get an understanding of the options available in this step.

- `wsdl2java`: Now, we start our Contract-first process. As we have the WSDL, we will use `wsdl2java` tools to create web service artifacts including the implementation template class. These generated files are placed in a folder, for example, `gensrc`. This step will also generate `deploy.wsdd` and `undeploy.wsdd`, two files which will help us generate server side deployment configurations later.

- `implement`: As mentioned previously, to avoid the manual process of adding code to the generated implementation template, we already have a Java file with the same name as the generated implementation template, which contains the same Java class, `HelloWebService`, with the business code implemented. So we will overwrite the generated file with the file already present, which in effect is equivalent to adding business code to the generated file.

- `compile`: We will now compile all the generated files, including the web service implementation class containing the business logic.

- `copy`: This will bring all required axis libraries to a staging directory for example, `lib` in our codebase, so that it is easy to package them into the web archive.

- `deploy`: In this step, we will use the `org.apache.axis.utils.Admin` class to generate the deployment configuration file, `server-config.wsdd`, taking `deploy.wsdd` as the input. We then create a standard web archive, which can be readily deployed into your favorite web server.

- `compileclient`: As a last step, we will compile the Client code too.

RpcClient.java

The `RpcClient` makes use of auto generated client side stub classes to invoke the remote web service in an RPC style.

```
public class RpcClient{
    private static String wsdlUrl = "http://localhost:8080/
                    AxisEndToEnd/services/HelloWebService?WSDL";
    private static String namespaceURI = "http://AxisEndToEnd.axis.
                    apache.binildas.com";
    private static String localPart = "IHelloWebService";
    protected void executeClient(String[] args)throws Exception{
        IHelloWebService iHelloWebService = null;
        IHelloWeb iHelloWeb = null;
        if(args.length == 3){
            iHelloWebService = new IHelloWebServiceLocator(args[0],
                new QName(args[1], args[2]));
        }
        else{
            iHelloWebService = new IHelloWebServiceLocator(wsdlUrl,
                new QName(namespaceURI, localPart));
        }
        iHelloWeb = iHelloWebService.getHelloWebService();
        log("Response From Server : " + iHelloWeb.hello("Binil"));
    }
```

```
        public static void main(String[] args)throws Exception{
            RpcClient client = new RpcClient();
            client.executeClient(args);
        }
    }
```

CallClient.java

We have provided one more client code called CallClient, which will use Axis and SOAP APIs to invoke the web service in a document oriented manner.

```
    public class CallClient {
        public static String wsURL =
            "http://localhost:8080/AxisEndToEnd/services/
HelloWebService?WSDL";
        public static String action = "HelloWebService";
        //SOAP Request - Not shown fully
        public static String msg = "<?xml version=\"1.0\"
            encoding=\"UTF-8\"?><soapenv:Envelope ...>";
        public static void test() throws Exception{
            InputStream input = new ByteArrayInputStream(msg.getBytes());
            Service service = new Service();
            Call call = (Call) service.createCall();
            SOAPEnvelope soapEnvelope = new SOAPEnvelope(input);
            call.setTargetEndpointAddress( new URL(wsURL) );
            if (action != null) {
                call.setUseSOAPAction( true );
                call.setSOAPActionURI( action );
            }
            soapEnvelope = call.invoke( soapEnvelope );
            System.out.println( "Response:\n" + soapEnvelope.toString() );
        }
        public static void main(String args[]) throws Exception{
            CallClient callClient = new CallClient();
            if(args.length > 0){
                wsURL = args[0];
            }
            if(args.length > 1){
                action = args[1];
            }
            callClient.test();
        }
    }
```

The document oriented web service request has not been fully shown in the code. But you can look at the source code to view it fully.

Run the Server and Client

The previous `build.xml` was a bit lengthy, and we again agree that the 10 steps mentioned earlier to implement the web service are not trivial ones for a novice user to execute. But believe it; we are going to do all those things with just one ant command. So, save the above `build.xml` file so that you can re-use them in your projects too.

To build the server side code, execute the following commands:

```
cd ch03\02_Axis
ant
```

The following figure shows the step-by-step execution of the build:

At the end of the build, we will have the deployable web archive (`AxisEndToEnd.war`) in the following location:

```
ch03\02_Axis\dist
```

You can now transfer this archive to the `webapps` folder of your web server and restart your server. Assuming the deployment went fine, the WSDL for the web service will be available now at the URL `http://localhost:8080/AxisEndToEnd/services/HelloWebService?WSDL`.

You can now execute the client code to test your web service. Since we have provided two versions of client code, there are two options for you to test the web service.

To execute the `RpcClient`, execute the following commands:

```
cd ch03\02_Axis
ant runrpc
```

The following figure shows the `RpcClient` execution console where it prints out any response received from the server:

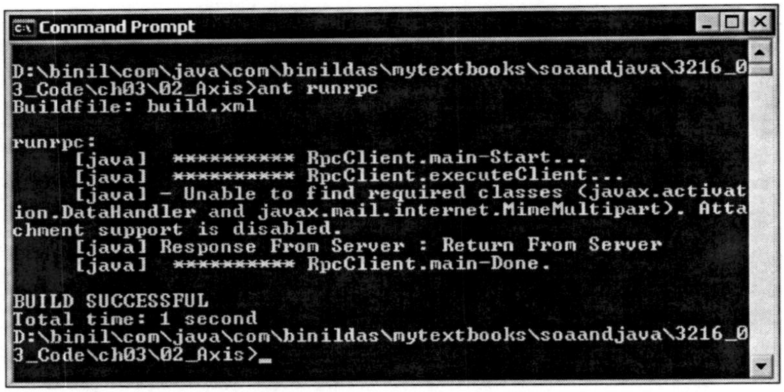

To execute the `CallClient`, execute the following commands:

```
cd ch03\02_Axis
ant runcall
```

The following figure shows the `RpcClient` execution console where it prints out any response received from the server:

```
Command Prompt                                              _ □ ×

D:\binil\com\java\com\binildas\mytextbooks\soaandjava\3216_0
3_Code\ch03\02_Axis>ant runcall
Buildfile: build.xml

runcall:
     [java] - Unable to find required classes (javax.activat
ion.DataHandler and javax.mail.internet.MimeMultipart). Atta
chment support is disabled.
     [java] Response:
     [java] <soapenv:Envelope xmlns:soapenv="http://schemas.
xmlsoap.org/soap/envelope/" xmlns:xsd="http://www.w3.org/200
1/XMLSchema" xmlns:xsi="http://www.w3.org/2001/XMLSchema-ins
tance"><soapenv:Body><ns1:helloResponse soapenv:encodingStyl
e="http://schemas.xmlsoap.org/soap/encoding/" xmlns:ns1="htt
p://AxisEndToEnd.axis.apache.binildas.com"><helloReturn xsi:
type="soapenc:string" xmlns:soapenc="http://schemas.xmlsoap.
org/soap/encoding/">Return From Server</helloReturn></ns1:he
lloResponse></soapenv:Body></soapenv:Envelope>

BUILD SUCCESSFUL
Total time: 1 second
D:\binil\com\java\com\binildas\mytextbooks\soaandjava\3216_0
3_Code\ch03\02_Axis>_
```

Web Service Using Spring

Spring has good support for Remoting. The main Remoting protocols Spring supports are RMI, HTTP-based Remoting (using `org.springframework.remoting.httpinvoker.HttpInvokerServiceExporter`), Hessian, Burlap, Spring support for SOAP, and Spring-WS (Web Services). Since this chapter is concentrating on web service implementations, let us look more into Spring support for SOAP and WS.

Spring-WS—A Primer

Spring-WS is available as a download different from core Spring from the site. Spring-WS support Contract-first style of WS development. Hence, the developers should be ready with the contract (WSDL) first to implement WS in Spring. This may not be trivial for every developer, especially for those who cannot create a WSDL by hand. The other alternative is to use some tools to author the contract, and then use Spring-WS for implementation.

We have already seen how to develop WS in Axis. Now, what we need more from Spring are its features such as:

- Dependency Injection
- Object Wiring

And for the reasons mentioned earlier, we also need a mechanism to generate or author the WSDL. Hence, to make the full process smooth and straightforward, we can use a mixed approach—using both Axis and Spring together so that we get best of both the worlds. We will see how to do that in this section.

Web Service Implementation in Spring

Since, we have already seen how to deploy an Axis web service, let us build on that to integrate Spring with the sample.

Spring provides `org.springframework.remoting.jaxrpc.ServletEndpointSupport`, which is a convenience base class for JAX-RPC servlet endpoint implementations. It provides a reference to the current Spring application context, so that we can do bean lookup or resource loading.

Code Server and Client

We will use the Server side codebase we have used for Axis sample with slight variations. Hence, the code is repeated in this section. The server side code artifacts are placed in the following folder ch03\03_Spring\WebService\src.

IHello.java

`IHello` is a simple business interface, with a single method `hello`. Since we want to share this interface with clients too, we have placed this interface alone in a common folder that is ch03\03_Spring\Common\src.

```
public interface IHello{
    String hello(String param);
}
```

IHelloWeb.java

Let us have an interface different from `IHello` to `IHelloWeb`, as our web service interface. So, we shall generate our contract out of this interface only.

```
public interface IHelloWeb extends IHello{
}
```

HelloWebService.java

Different from our Axis sample, `HelloWebService` here extends `ServletEndpointSupport`, so that we get a reference to the current Spring application context.

```
public class HelloWebService extends ServletEndpointSupport implements
IHelloWeb{
    private IHello iHello;
    public HelloWebService(){
        System.out.println("Inside HelloWebService.HelloWebService...");
    }
    protected void onInit() {
        System.out.println("Inside HelloWebService.onInit...");
        this.iHello = (IHello) getWebApplicationContext().
getBean("hello");
    }
    public void setHello(IHello iHello){
        this.iHello = iHello;
    }
    public String hello(String param){
        System.out.println("Inside HelloWebService.hello...");
        return iHello.hello(param);
    }
}
```

Here in the onInit method, we get a reference to Spring context to resolve the bean with the name, hello. This bean refers to a different business bean, where we implement our business code which is explained next.

Hello.java

Hello is a spring bean, which we configure in the applicationContext.xml. This bean implements the business method.

```
public class Hello implements IHello{
    public Hello(){
        System.out.println("Inside Hello.Hello...");
    }
    public String hello(String param){
        System.out.println("Inside Hello.hello...");
        return "Hello " + param;
    }
}
```

applicationContext.xml

The `applicationContext.xml` will have definitions of all Spring beans, and is placed in the folder `ch03\03_Spring\WebService\config`.

```xml
<?xml version="1.0" encoding="UTF-8"?>
<!DOCTYPE beans PUBLIC "-//SPRING//DTD BEAN//EN" "http://www.
springframework.org/dtd/spring-beans.dtd">
<beans>
    <bean id="hello" class="com.binildas.apache.axis.AxisSpring.Hello">
    </bean>
</beans>
```

web.xml

The `web.xml` placed in `ch03\03_Spring\WebService\config` will explain how we can hook the Spring context to the current web application context. When we package the web archive, we need to place the `applicationContext.xml` in the path specified in the `web.xml` (/WEB-INF/).

```xml
<?xml version="1.0" encoding="ISO-8859-1"?>
<!DOCTYPE web-app PUBLIC "-//Sun Microsystems, Inc.//DTD Web
Application 2.3//EN" "http://java.sun.com/dtd/web-app_2_3.dtd">
<web-app>
    <listener>
        <listener-class>
            org.springframework.web.context.ContextLoaderListener
        </listener-class>
    </listener>
    <context-param>
        <param-name>contextConfigLocation</param-name>
        <param-value>
            /WEB-INF/applicationContext.xml
        </param-value>
    </context-param>
    <servlet>
        <servlet-name>AxisServlet</servlet-name>
        <display-name>Apache-Axis Servlet</display-name>
        <servlet-class>
            org.apache.axis.transport.http.AxisServlet
        </servlet-class>
        <load-on-startup>1</load-on-startup>
    </servlet>
    <servlet-mapping>
```

```
        <servlet-name>AxisServlet</servlet-name>
        <url-pattern>/services/*</url-pattern>
    </servlet-mapping>
</web-app>
```

Client.java

Let us code the client too using Spring features, in a simple manner. Look at the code to know how we can do that.

```java
public class Client{
    private ApplicationContext ctx;
    private ClientObject clientObject;
    public Client(){
        String[] paths = {"/applicationContextClient.xml"};
        ctx = new ClassPathXmlApplicationContext(paths);
        clientObject = (ClientObject) ctx.getBean("clientObject");
    }
    public void finalize()throws Throwable{
        super.finalize();
        clientObject = null;
        ctx = null;
    }
    private void test1(){
        log(clientObject.hello("Binil"));
    }
    public static void main(String[] args)throws Exception{
        Client client = new Client();
        client.test1();
    }
}
```

The Client makes use of another spring bean, ClientObject. We wire this bean in a second Spring configuration file, applicationContextClient.xml.

ClientObject.java

The ClientObject is just a helper bean.

```java
public class ClientObject{
    private IHello helloService;
    public void setHelloService(IHello helloService) {
        this.helloService = helloService;
    }
    public String hello(String param) {
        return helloService.hello(param);
    }
}
```

We inject a proxy to the remote web service into this bean. So, any calls can be delegated to the web service. The proxy configuration and wiring is done in `applicationContextClient.xml`.

applicationContextClient.xml

In `applicationContextClient.xml`, we configure both the `ClientObject` bean and a proxy to the remote web service. To configure the proxy, you define a `JaxRpcPortProxyFactoryBean` so that the proxy will implement the remote interface. As you have chosen Axis to implement your Spring-based web service, we will use Axis itself for the client side invocation too. So you must specify `org.apache.axis.client.ServiceFactory` as the service factory class to use. Then you also define other parameters for the `JaxRpcPortProxyFactoryBean` as shown in following code listing:

```xml
<?xml version="1.0" encoding="UTF-8"?>
<!DOCTYPE beans PUBLIC "-//SPRING//DTD BEAN//EN"
"http://www.springframework.org/dtd/spring-beans.dtd">
<beans>
    <bean id="helloService" class="org.springframework.remoting.jaxrpc.
JaxRpcPortProxyFactoryBean">
        <property name="serviceFactoryClass">
            <value>org.apache.axis.client.ServiceFactory</value>
        </property>
        <property name="serviceInterface"
            value="com.binildas.apache.axis.AxisSpring.IHello"/>
        <property name="wsdlDocumentUrl"
            value="http://localhost:8080/AxisSpring/
                services/HelloWebService?wsdl"/>
        <property name="namespaceUri"
            value="http://AxisSpring.axis.apache.binildas.com"/>
        <property name="serviceName" value="IHelloWebService"/>
        <property name="portName" value="HelloWebService"/>
    </bean>
    <bean id="clientObject"
        class="com.binildas.apache.axis.AxisSpring.ClientObject">
        <property name="helloService" ref="helloService"/>
    </bean>
</beans>
```

Run the Server and Client

To build the server side code, execute the following commands:

```
cd ch03\03_Spring
ant
```

The above command will build both the server and the client codebase. At the end of the build, we will have the deployable web archive (AxisSpring.war) in the following location:

```
ch03\03_Spring\WebService\dist
```

You can now transfer this archive to the webapps folder of your web server and restart your server. Assuming the deployment went fine, the WSDL for the web service will be available now at the URL http://localhost:8080/AxisSpring/services/HelloWebService?wsdl.

You can now execute the clients' code to test your web service. To execute the Client, execute the following commands:

```
cd ch03\03_Spring
ant run
```

The following figure shows the client side screenshot:

Web Service Using XFire

XFire is a new generation Java SOAP framework. XFire API is easy to use, and supports standards. Hence XFire makes SOA development much easier and straightforward. XFire is also highly performance oriented, since it is built on a low memory **StAX (Streaming API for XML)** model. Currently, XFire is available in version 2.0 under the name CXF.

Web Service Implementation in XFire

You have already seen implementing web services in Axis and Spring, by creating standard web archives and deploying them into web servers. Now, we will do a similar exercise here, but in a relatively lightweight manner, using XFire. Here, we assume you have already downloaded XFire 1.2.2 version from the URL `http://xfire.codehaus.org/Download`, and have extracted it to the folder which you can refer to in your `examples.PROPERTIES` file as `xfire.home`.

Code Server and Client

For our XFire sample, we have all the code organized in the folder `ch03\04_XFire\src`. We will now look at them, one by one.

IHello.java

As usual, `IHello` is a simple Java business interface, defining a single method `sayHello`.

```
public interface IHello{
    String sayHello(String name);
}
```

HelloServiceImpl

`HelloServiceImpl` is our web service implementation class, implementing `IHello` interface.

```
public class HelloServiceImpl implements IHello{
    private static long times = 0L;
    public HelloServiceImpl(){
        System.out.println("HelloServiceImpl.HelloServiceImpl()...");
    }
    public String sayHello(String name){
        System.out.println("HelloServiceImpl.sayHello
                        (" + (++times) + ")");
        return "HelloServiceImpl.sayHello :
                        HELLO! You just said:" + name;
    }
}
```

web.xml

For XFire web services, we need to set up `org.codehaus.xfire.transport.http.XFireConfigurableServlet` as the Servlet. We then route all URL requests of pattern `/services/` to `XFireConfigurableServlet` as shown in the `web.xml`.

```xml
<?xml version="1.0" encoding="ISO-8859-1"?>
<!DOCTYPE web-app
    PUBLIC "-//Sun Microsystems, Inc.//DTD Web Application 2.3//EN"
    "http://java.sun.com/dtd/web-app_2_3.dtd">
<web-app>

    <servlet>
        <servlet-name>XFireServlet</servlet-name>
        <display-name>XFire Servlet</display-name>
        <servlet-class>
            org.codehaus.xfire.transport.http.XFireConfigurableServlet
        </servlet-class>
    </servlet>

    <servlet-mapping>
        <servlet-name>XFireServlet</servlet-name>
        <url-pattern>/servlet/XFireServlet/*</url-pattern>
    </servlet-mapping>

    <servlet-mapping>
        <servlet-name>XFireServlet</servlet-name>
        <url-pattern>/services/*</url-pattern>
    </servlet-mapping>

</web-app>
```

services.xml

The `services.xml` is the main XFire configuration file. Let us look into the sample file and understand it in detail.

```xml
<beans xmlns="http://xfire.codehaus.org/config/1.0">
    <service>
        <name>Hello</name>
        <namespace>http://xfire.binildas.com</namespace>
        <serviceClass>com.binildas.xfire.IHello</serviceClass>
        <implementationClass>
            com.binildas.xfire.HelloServiceImpl
        </implementationClass>
    </service>
</beans>
```

The `name` element is required and denotes the name of the service as exposed to the world. The optional `namespace` element specifies the target namespace for the service. The `serviceClass` denotes the name of the object you wish to make into a service, whereas the `implementationClass` denotes the implementation which you wish to use when the service is invoked.

Run the Server and Client

To build the server side code, execute the following commands:

```
cd ch03\04_XFire
ant
```

The above command will build both the server and the client codebase. At the end of the build, we will have the deployable web archive (HelloXFire.war) in the following location:

```
ch03\04_XFire\dist
```

You can now transfer this archive to the webapps folder of your web server and restart your server. Assuming the deployment went fine, the WSDL for the web service will be available now at the URL http://localhost:8080/HelloXFire/services/Hello?wsdl.

You can now execute the clients' code to test your web service. To execute the Client code, execute the following commands:

```
cd ch03\04_XFire
ant run
```

The following figure shows the client side screenshot:

```
Command Prompt                                          _ □ X

D:\binil\com\java\com\binildas\mytextbooks\soaandjava\3216_0
3_Code\ch03\04_XFire>ant run
Buildfile: build.xml

run:
     [java] Client.main : Start...
     [java] Client.main : Start...
     [java] callSoapServiceLocal(): got service model.
     [java] Client.main : End. status = HelloServiceImpl.say
Hello : HELLO! You just said: Sowmya
     [java] Response from WEB SERVICE: HelloServiceImpl.sayH
ello : HELLO! You just said: Sowmya
     [java] Client.main : End.

BUILD SUCCESSFUL
Total time: 1 second
D:\binil\com\java\com\binildas\mytextbooks\soaandjava\3216_0
3_Code\ch03\04_XFire>_
```

Summary

In this chapter, we concentrated on major web services implementation available in the Java world, and while doing all this we covered the following:

- **JAX-WS 2.0**: JAX-WS 2.0 is the reference implementation of the Java API for XML web services (JAX-WS) specification. We have seen samples in JAX-WS which can be deployed in Java EE Application Server or into Java SE 6.

- **Apache Axis**: Axis is Apache open-source web service implementation with many production deployments. We have seen a full-service deployment, where we package the code artifacts into a standard web archive and then deploy them into Apache Tomcat web server.

- **Spring**: Spring provides dependency injection and bean wiring along with other features, and we can develop web services using Spring core or Sring-WS. The sample, in this chapter, uses Spring core to enhance the Axis web service sample.

- **Xfire**: Xfire is a new generation Java SOAP framework, which is easier and straightforward for developing web services. The Xfire sample provided, demonstrates how easy it is to build and deploy web services using Xfire.

4
Data and Services—All Roads Lead to Enterprise Service Bus

Having seen the basics of XML and XML-based services in the previous chapters, we are now ready to look into the big picture of enterprise landscape and see how all the pieces fit together. What is of interest for every enterprise user is information and every information starts from the basic building block, data. Data can reside in any data store, and can exist in many formats. Irrespective of that, you need to bring data to your table, do some massaging with your business use cases, and supply them as information. How do we do that in the SOA world, moving away from the traditional JDBC or **Object-relational mapping (OR mapping)** styles? And more interesting is, data can even exist in the form of services and if so, how do we combine multiple services just like we combine data from multiple JDBC query results? We are going to look at a couple of these aspects in this chapter, and we will cover specifically:

- JDO as an alternative to JDBC
- Data Services and its role in SOA
- Few emerging Data Services standards like SCA and SDO
- Introducing Apache Tuscany
- Introduction to message-oriented middleware (MOM)
- Enterprise Service Bus (ESB)—The new architecture style
- Introducing OpenESB

JDO

You all are perfectly comfortable with JDBC or few OR-mapping frameworks at least, like Hibernate or TopLink. Let us now look into a complementing standard of accessing data from your data store using a standard interface-based abstraction model of persistence in java that is, **Java Data Objects (JDO)**. The original JDO (JDO 1.0) specification is quite old and is based on **Java Specification Request 12 (JSR 12)**. The current major version of JDO (JDO 2.0) is based on JSR 243. The original specifications were done under the supervision of Sun and starting from 2.0, the development of the API and the reference implementation happens as an Apache open-source project.

Why JDO?

We have been happily programming to retrieve data from relational stores using JDBC, and now the big question is do we need yet another standard, JDO? If you think that as software programmers you need to provide solutions to your business problems, it makes sense for you to start with the business use cases and then do a business analysis at the end of which you will come out with a **Business Domain Object Model (BDOM)**. The BDOM will drive the design of your entity classes, which are to be persisted to a suitable data store. Once you design your entity classes and their relationship, the next question is should you be writing code to create tables, and persist or query data from these tables (or data stores, if there are no tables). I would like to answer 'No' for this question, since the more code you write, the more are the chances of making errors, and further, developer time is costly. Moreover, today you may write JDBC for doing the above mentioned "technical functionalities", and tomorrow you may want to change all your JDBC to some other standard since you want to port your data from a relational store to a different persistence mechanism. To sum up, let us list down a few of the features of JDO which distinguishes itself from other similar frameworks.

- **Separation of Concerns**: Application developers can focus on the BDOM and leave the persistence details (storage and retrieval) to the JDO implementation.
- **API-based**: JDO is based on a java interface-based programming model. Hence all persistence behavior including most commonly used features of OR mapping is available as metadata, external to your BDOM source code. We can also Plug and Play (PnP) multiple JDO implementations, which know how to interact well with the underlying data store.

- **Data store portability**: Irrespective of whether the persistent store is a relational or object-based file, or just an XML DB or a flat file, JDO implementations can still support the code. Hence, JDO applications are independent of the underlying database.

- **Performance**: A specific JDO implementation knows how to interact better with its specific data store, which will improve performance as compared to developer written code.

- **J2EE integration**: JDO applications can take advantage of J2EE features like EJB and thus the enterprise features such as remote message processing, automatic distributed transaction coordination, security, and so on.

JPOX—Java Persistent Objects

JPOX is an Apache open-source project, which aims at a heterogeneous persistence solution for Java using JDO. By heterogeneous we mean, JPOX JDO will support any combination of the following four main aspects of persistence:

- **Persistence Definition**: The mechanism of defining how your BDOM classes are to be persisted to the data store.

- **Persistence API**: The programming API used to persist your BDOM objects.

- **Query Language**: The language used to find objects due to certain criteria.

- **Data store**: The underlying persistent store you are persisting your objects to.

JPOX JDO is available for download at http://www.jpox.org/.

JDO Sample Using JPOX

In this sample, we will take the familiar Order and LineItems scenario, and expand it to have a JDO implementation. It is assumed that you have already downloaded and extracted the JPOX libraries to your local hard drive.

BDOM for the Sample

We will limit our BDOM for the sample discussion to just two entity classes, that is, `OrderList` and `LineItem`. The class attributes and relationships are shown in the following screenshot:

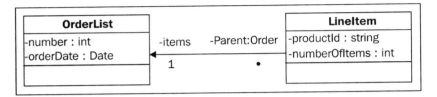

The BDOM illustrates that an Order can contain multiple line items. Conversely, each line item is related to one and only one Order.

Code BDOM Entities for JDO

The BDOM classes are simple entity classes with `getter` and `setter` methods for each attribute. These classes are then required to be wired for JDO persistence capability in a JDO specific configuration file, which is completely external to the core entity classes.

OrderList.java

`OrderList` is the class representing the Order, and is having a primary key attribute that is `number`.

```
public class OrderList{
    private int number;
    private Date orderDate;
    private Set lineItems;
    // other getter & setter methods go here
    // Inner class for composite PK
    public static class Oid implements Serializable{
        public int number;
        public Oid(){
        }
        public Oid(int param){
            this.number = param;
        }
        public String toString(){
```

```
         return String.valueOf(number);
      }
      public int hashCode(){
         return number;
      }
      public boolean equals(Object other){
         if (other != null && (other instanceof Oid)){
            Oid k = (Oid)other;
            return k.number == this.number;
         }
         return false;
      }
   }
}
```

LineItem.java

`LineItem` represents each item container in the Order. We don't explicitly define a primary key for `LineItem` even though JDO will have its own mechanism to do that.

```
public class LineItem{
   private String productId;
   private int numberOfItems;
   private OrderList orderList;
   // other getter & setter methods go here
}
```

package.jdo

JDO requires an XML configuration file, which defines the fields that are to be persisted and to what JDBC or JDO wrapper constructs should be mapped to. For this, we can create an XML file called `package.jdo` with the following content and put it in the same directory where we have the entities.

```
<?xml version="1.0" encoding="UTF-8"?>
<!DOCTYPE jdo SYSTEM "file:/javax/jdo/jdo.dtd">
<jdo>
   <package name="com.binildas.jdo.jpox.order">
      <class name="OrderList" identity-type="application"
          objectid-class="OrderList$Oid" table="ORDERLIST">
         <field name="number" primary-key="true">
           <column name="ORDERLIST_ID"/>
         </field>
         <field name="orderDate">
```

```
                    <column name="ORDER_DATE"/>
            </field>
            <field name="lineItems" persistence-modifier="persistent"
                    mapped-by="orderList">
                <collection element-type="LineItem">
                </collection>
            </field>
        </class>
        <class name="LineItem" table="LINEITEM">
            <field name="productId">
                <column name="PRODUCT_ID"/>
            </field>
            <field name="numberOfItems">
                <column name="NUMBER_OF_ITEMS"/>
            </field>
            <field name="orderList" persistence-modifier="persistent">
                <column name="LINEITEM_ORDERLIST_ID"/>
            </field>
        </class>
    </package>
</jdo>
```

jpox.PROPERTIES

In this sample, we will persist our entities to a relational database, Oracle. We specify the main connection parameters in jpox.PROPERTIES file.

```
javax.jdo.PersistenceManagerFactoryClass=org.jpox.jdo.
JDOPersistenceManagerFactory

javax.jdo.option.ConnectionDriverName=oracle.jdbc.driver.OracleDriver
javax.jdo.option.ConnectionURL=jdbc:oracle:thin:@127.0.0.1:1521:orcl
javax.jdo.option.ConnectionUserName=scott
javax.jdo.option.ConnectionPassword=tiger

org.jpox.autoCreateSchema=true
org.jpox.validateTables=false
org.jpox.validateConstraints=false
```

Main.java

This class contains the code to test the JDO functionalities. As shown here, it creates two Orders and adds few line items to each order. First it persists these entities and then queries back these entities using the id.

```java
public class Main{
    static public void main(String[] args){
        Properties props = new Properties();
        try{
            props.load(new FileInputStream("jpox.properties"));
        }
        catch (Exception e){
            e.printStackTrace();
        }
        PersistenceManagerFactory pmf =
            JDOHelper.getPersistenceManagerFactory(props);
        PersistenceManager pm = pmf.getPersistenceManager();
        Transaction tx = pm.currentTransaction();
        Object id = null;
        try{
            tx.begin();
            LineItem lineItem1 = new LineItem("CD011", 1);
            LineItem lineItem2 = new LineItem("CD022", 2);
            OrderList orderList = new OrderList(1, new Date());
            orderList.getLineItems().add(lineItem1);
            orderList.getLineItems().add(lineItem2);

            LineItem lineItem3 = new LineItem("CD033", 3);
            LineItem lineItem4 = new LineItem("CD044", 4);
            OrderList orderList2 = new OrderList(2, new Date());
            orderList2.getLineItems().add(lineItem3);
            orderList2.getLineItems().add(lineItem4);

            pm.makePersistent(orderList);
            id = pm.getObjectId(orderList);
            System.out.println("Persisted id : "+ id);

            pm.makePersistent(orderList2);
            id = pm.getObjectId(orderList2);
            System.out.println("Persisted id : "+ id);

            orderList = (OrderList) pm.getObjectById(id);
            System.out.println("Retreived orderList : " + orderList);
            tx.commit();
```

```
            }
        catch (Exception e){
            e.printStackTrace();
            if (tx.isActive()){
                tx.rollback();
            }
        }
        finally{
            pm.close();
        }
    }
}
```

Build and Run the JDO Sample

As a first step, if you haven't done it before, edit `examples.PROPERTIES` provided along with the code download for this chapter and change the paths there to match your development environment. The code download for this chapter also includes a `README.txt` file, which gives detailed steps to build and run the samples.

Since we use Oracle to persist entities, we need the following two libraries in the `classpath`:

- jpox-rdbms*.jar
- classes12.jar

We require a couple of other libraries too which are specified in the `build.xml` file. Download these libraries and change the path in `examples.PROPERTIES` accordingly.

To build the sample, first bring up your database server. Then to build the sample in a single command, it is easy for you to go to `ch04\jdo` folder and execute the following command.

```
cd ch04\jdo
ant
```

The above command will execute the following steps:

- First it compiles the java source files
- Then for every class you persist, use JPOX libraries to enhance the byte code.
- As the last step, we create the required schema in the data store.

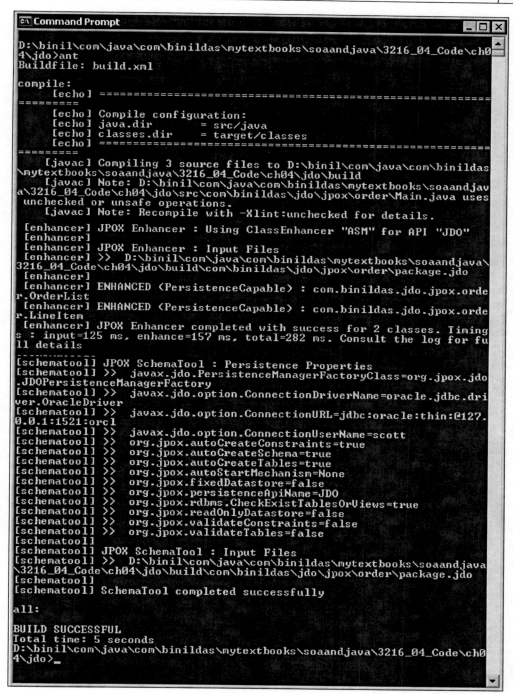

```
D:\binil\com\java\com\binildas\mytextbooks\soaandjava\3216_04_Code\ch0
4\jdo>ant
Buildfile: build.xml

compile:
    [echo] ===========================================================
=========
    [echo] Compile configuration:
    [echo] java.dir          = src/java
    [echo] classes.dir       = target/classes
    [echo] ===========================================================
=========
    [javac] Compiling 3 source files to D:\binil\com\java\com\binildas
\mytextbooks\soaandjava\3216_04_Code\ch04\jdo\build
    [javac] Note: D:\binil\com\java\com\binildas\mytextbooks\soaandjav
a\3216_04_Code\ch04\jdo\src\com\binildas\jdo\jpox\order\Main.java uses
unchecked or unsafe operations.
    [javac] Note: Recompile with -Xlint:unchecked for details.

  [enhancer] JPOX Enhancer : Using ClassEnhancer "ASM" for API "JDO"
  [enhancer]
  [enhancer] JPOX Enhancer : Input Files
  [enhancer] >>  D:\binil\com\java\com\binildas\mytextbooks\soaandjava\
3216_04_Code\ch04\jdo\build\com\binildas\jdo\jpox\order\package.jdo
  [enhancer]
  [enhancer] ENHANCED (PersistenceCapable) : com.binildas.jdo.jpox.orde
r.OrderList
  [enhancer] ENHANCED (PersistenceCapable) : com.binildas.jdo.jpox.orde
r.LineItem
  [enhancer] JPOX Enhancer completed with success for 2 classes. Timing
s : input=125 ms, enhance=157 ms, total=282 ms. Consult the log for fu
ll details
------------
[schematool] JPOX SchemaTool : Persistence Properties
[schematool] >>  javax.jdo.PersistenceManagerFactoryClass=org.jpox.jdo
.JDOPersistenceManagerFactory
[schematool] >>  javax.jdo.option.ConnectionDriverName=oracle.jdbc.dri
ver.OracleDriver
[schematool] >>  javax.jdo.option.ConnectionURL=jdbc:oracle:thin:@127.
0.0.1:1521:orcl
[schematool] >>  javax.jdo.option.ConnectionUserName=scott
[schematool] >>  org.jpox.autoCreateConstraints=true
[schematool] >>  org.jpox.autoCreateSchema=true
[schematool] >>  org.jpox.autoCreateTables=true
[schematool] >>  org.jpox.autoStartMechanism=None
[schematool] >>  org.jpox.fixedDatastore=false
[schematool] >>  org.jpox.persistenceApiName=JDO
[schematool] >>  org.jpox.rdbms.CheckExistTablesOrViews=true
[schematool] >>  org.jpox.readOnlyDatastore=false
[schematool] >>  org.jpox.validateConstraints=false
[schematool] >>  org.jpox.validateTables=false
[schematool]
[schematool] JPOX SchemaTool : Input Files
[schematool] >>  D:\binil\com\java\com\binildas\mytextbooks\soaandjava
\3216_04_Code\ch04\jdo\build\com\binildas\jdo\jpox\order\package.jdo
[schematool]
[schematool] SchemaTool completed successfully

all:

BUILD SUCCESSFUL
Total time: 5 seconds
D:\binil\com\java\com\binildas\mytextbooks\soaandjava\3216_04_Code\ch0
4\jdo>_
```

To run the sample, execute:

```
ant run
```

You can now cross check whether the entities are persisted to your data store. This is as shown in the following screenshot where you can see that each line item is related to the parent order by the foreign key.

Data Services

Good that you now know how to manage the basic data operations in a generic way using JDO and other techniques. By now, you also have good hands-on experience in defining and deploying web services. We all appreciate that web services are functionalities exposed in standard, platform, and technology neutral way. When we say functionality we mean the business use cases translated in the form of useful information. Information is always processed out of data. So, once we retrieve data, we need to process it to translate them into information.

When we define SOA strategies at an enterprise level, we deal with multiple **Line of Business (LOB)** systems; some of them will be dealing with the same kind of business entity. For example, a customer entity is required for a CRM system as well as for a sales or marketing system. This necessitates a **Common Data Model (CDM)**, which is often referred to as the Canonical Data Model or Information Model. In such a model, you will often have entities that represent "domain" concepts, for example, customer, account, address, order, and so on. So, multiple LOB systems will make use of these domain entities in different ways, seeking different information-based on the business context. OK, now we are in a position to introduce the next concept in SOA, which is "Data Services".

Data Services are specialization of web services which are data and information oriented. They need to manage the traditional **CRUD (Create, Read, Update,** and **Delete)** operations as well as a few other data functionalities such as search and information modeling. The Create operation will give you back a unique ID whereas Read, Update, and Delete operations are performed on a specific unique ID. Search will usually be done with some form of search criteria and information modeling, or retrieval happens when we pull useful information out of the CDM, for example, retrieving the address for a customer.

The next important thing is that no assumptions should be made that the data will be in a java resultset form or in a collection of transfer object form. Instead, you are now dealing with data in SOA context and it makes sense to visualize data in XML format. Hence, **XML Schema Definition (XSDs)** can be used to define the format of your requests and responses for each of these canonical data definitions. You may also want to use ad hoc queries using XQuery or XPath expressions, similar to SQL capabilities on relational data. In other words, your data retrieval and data recreation for information processing at your middle tier should support XML tools and mechanisms, and should also support the above six basic data operations. If so, higher level of abstractions in the processing tier can make use of the above data services to provide Application Specialization capabilities, specialized for the LOB systems. To make the concept clear, let us assume that we need to get the order status for a particular customer (`getCustomerOrderStatus()`) which will take the customer ID argument. The data services layer will have a retrieve operation passing the customer ID and the XQuery or the XPath statement will obtain the requested order information from the retrieved customer data. High level processing layers (such as LOB service tiers) can use high-level interface (for example, our `getCustomerOrderStatus` operation) of the Application Specialization using a web services (data services) interface and need not know or use XQuery or XPath directly. The underlying XQuery or XPath can be encapsulated, reused, and optimized.

Service Data Objects

Data abstraction and unified data access are the two main concerns that any SOA-based architecture has to address. In the data services discussion, we talked a bit about data abstraction, by first defining data around domain entities and then decorating it with useful methods for data operations. Equally important is the issue of accessing heterogeneous data in a uniform way.

Why SDO?

One of the main problems **Service Data Objects (SDO)** tries to solve is the issue of heterogeneous manner of data management. By data management, we mean data storage as well as operations on data lifecycle. SDO simplifies J2EE data programming model thus giving application developers more time to focus on the business problems.

SDO provides developers an API, the SDO API, and a programming model to access data. This API lets you to work with data from heterogeneous data sources, including RDBMS, entity EJBs, XML sources, web services, EIS data sources using the Java Connector Architecture, and so on. Hence you as a developer need not be familiar with a technology-specific API such as JDBC or XQuery in order to access and utilize data. Instead, you can just use SDO API.

SDO Architecture

In SDO, data is organized as a graph of objects, called `DataObject`. A `DataObject` is the fundamental component which is a representation of some structured data, with some properties. These properties have either a single value or multiple values, and their values can be even other data objects. Each data objects also maintains a change summary, which represents the alterations made to it.

SDO clients or consumers always use SDO programming model and API. This is generic of technology and framework, and hence the developers need not know how the underlying data they are working with is persisted. A **Data Mediator Service (DMS)** is responsible for creating a data graph from data source(s), and also for updating the data source(s) based on any changes made to a data graph. SDO clients are disconnected from both the DMS and the data source.

A DMS will create a **Data Graph**, which is a container for a tree of data objects. Another interesting fact is that a single data graph can represent data from different data sources. This is actually a design model to deal with data aggregation scenarios from multiple data sources. The data graphs form the basics of the disconnected architecture of SDO, since they can be passed across layers and tiers in an application. When doing so, they are serialized to the XML format.

A **Change Summary** contains any change information related to the data in the data object. Change summaries are initially empty and are populated as and when the data graph is modified.

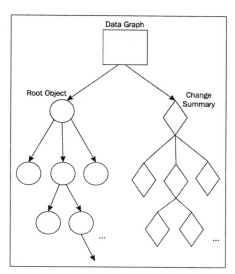

Apache Tuscany SDO

Apache Tuscany SDO is a sub-project within open-source Apache Tuscany.

Apache Tuscany aims at defining an infrastructure that simplifies the development of Service-Oriented application networks, addressing real business problems. It is based on specifications defined by the **OASIS Open Composite Services Architecture (CSA) Member Section**, which advances open standards that simplify SOA application development.

Tuscany SDO mainly provides implementations in Java and C++. Both are available for download at: `http://incubator.apache.org/tuscany/`.

SDO Sample Using Tuscany SDO

SDO can handle heterogeneous data sources, but for the sample here, we will make use of an XML file as a data source. The sample will read as well as write an XML file, when the client program makes use of SDO API to do data operations.

Code the Sample Artifacts

The main artifacts for running the samples in SDO include an XSD schema file and an XML instance file. Then we have two java programs, one which reads the XML and another which creates an XML. We will look into these files first.

hr.xsd

The `hr.xsd` restricts the structure of an employee XML file, which can contain multiple employees. Each employee can have a name, address, organization, and office elements. Each of these elements can have sub-elements, which are as shown here:

```
<?xml version="1.0"?>
<xsd:schema xmlns:xsd="http://www.w3.org/2001/XMLSchema"
xmlns="http://www.binildas.com/apache/tuscany/sdo/sample"
targetNamespace="http://www.binildas.com/apache/tuscany/sdo/sample">
    <xsd:element name="employees">
        <xsd:complexType>
            <xsd:sequence>
                <xsd:element ref="employee" maxOccurs="unbounded" />
            </xsd:sequence>
        </xsd:complexType>
    </xsd:element>
    <xsd:element name="employee">
        <xsd:annotation>
            <xsd:documentation>Employee
                    representation</xsd:documentation>
        </xsd:annotation>
        <xsd:complexType>
            <xsd:sequence>
                <xsd:element name="name" type="xsd:string" />
                <xsd:element ref="address" maxOccurs="2" />
                <xsd:element ref="organization" />
                <xsd:element ref="office" />
```

```
        </xsd:sequence>
        <xsd:attribute name="id" type="xsd:integer" />
    </xsd:complexType>
</xsd:element>
<xsd:element name="organization">
    <xsd:complexType>
        <xsd:sequence>
            <xsd:element name="name" type="xsd:string"/>
        </xsd:sequence>
        <xsd:attribute name="id" type="xsd:integer" />
    </xsd:complexType>
</xsd:element>
<xsd:element name="office">
    <xsd:complexType>
        <xsd:sequence>
            <xsd:element ref="address"/>
        </xsd:sequence>
        <xsd:attribute name="id" type="xsd:integer" />
    </xsd:complexType>
</xsd:element>
<xsd:element name="address">
    <xsd:complexType>
        <xsd:sequence>
            <xsd:element name="street1" type="xsd:string"/>
            <xsd:element name="street2" type="xsd:string"
                    minOccurs="0"/>
            <xsd:element name="city" type="xsd:string"/>
            <xsd:element name="state" type="stateAbbreviation"/>
            <xsd:element ref="zip-code"/>
        </xsd:sequence>
    </xsd:complexType>
</xsd:element>
<xsd:element name="zip-code">
    <xsd:simpleType>
        <xsd:restriction base="xsd:string">
            <xsd:pattern value="[0-9]{5}(-[0-9]{4})?"/>
        </xsd:restriction>
    </xsd:simpleType>
</xsd:element>
<xsd:simpleType name="stateAbbreviation">
    <xsd:restriction base="xsd:string">
        <xsd:pattern value="[A-Z]{2}"/>
    </xsd:restriction>
</xsd:simpleType>
</xsd:schema>
```

hr.xml

The `hr.xml` provided is fully constrained as per the above schema. For our sample demonstration this XML file contains data on two employees as shown here:

```xml
<?xml version="1.0"?>
<employees xmlns="http://www.binildas.com/apache/tuscany/sdo/sample">
  <employee id="30379">
    <name>Binildas C. A.</name>
    <address>
      <street1>45 Bains Compound Nanthencode</street1>
      <city>Trivandrum</city>
      <state>KL</state>
      <zip-code>695003</zip-code>
    </address>
    <organization id="08">
      <name>Software</name>
    </organization>
    <office id="31">
      <address>
        <street1>101 Camarino Ruiz</street1>
        <street2>Apt 2 Camarillo</street2>
        <city>Callifornia</city>
        <state>LA</state>
        <zip-code>93012</zip-code>
      </address>
    </office>
  </employee>
  <employee id="30380">
    <name>Rajesh R V</name>
    <address>
      <street1>1400 Salt Lake Road</street1>
      <street2>Appartment 5E</street2>
      <city>Boston</city>
      <state>MA</state>
      <zip-code>20967</zip-code>
    </address>
    <organization id="15">
      <name>Research</name>
    </organization>
    <office id="21">
      <address>
        <street1>2700 Cambridge Drive</street1>
        <city>Boston</city>
        <state>MA</state>
```

```
            <zip-code>20968</zip-code>
          </address>
        </office>
      </employee>
    </employees>
```

ReadEmployees.java

Now, we are going to see SDO in action. In the ReadEmployees class shown below, we first read the XML file, mentioned previously, and load it into a root DataObject. A DataObject is a graph of other DataObjects. Hence, we can iterate over the graph and get each item DataObject.

```java
public class ReadEmployees extends SampleBase{
    private static final String HR_XML_RESOURCE = "hr.xml";
    public static final String HR_XSD_RESOURCE = "hr.xsd";
    public ReadEmployees(Integer commentaryLevel) {
        super(commentaryLevel,
                SampleInfrastructure.SAMPLE_LEVEL_BASIC);
    }
    public static void main(String[] args)throws Exception{
        ReadEmployees sample = new
                            ReadEmployees(COMMENTARY_FOR_NOVICE);
        sample.runSample();
    }
    public void runSample () throws Exception{
        InputStream inputStream =
            ClassLoader.getSystemResourceAsStream(HR_XML_RESOURCE);
        byte[] bytes = new byte[inputStream.available()];
        inputStream.read(bytes);
        inputStream.close();
        HelperContext scope = createScopeForTypes();
        loadTypesFromXMLSchemaFile(scope, HR_XSD_RESOURCE);
        XMLDocument xmlDoc = getXMLDocumentFromString(scope,
            new String(bytes));
        DataObject purchaseOrder = xmlDoc.getRootObject();
        List itemList = purchaseOrder.getList("employee");
        DataObject item = null;
        for (int i = 0; i < itemList.size(); i++) {
            item = (DataObject) itemList.get(i);
            System.out.println("id: " + item.get("id"));
            System.out.println("name: " + item.get("name"));
        }
    }
}
```

CreateEmployees.java

In the `CreateEmployees` class, we do the reverse process — we define `DataObjects` in code and build the SDO graph. At the end, the root `DataObject` is persisted to a file and also to the system output stream as shown in the following code.

```
public class CreateEmployees extends SampleBase {
    private static final String HR_XML_RESOURCE_NEW = "hr_new.xml";
    public static final String HR_XSD_RESOURCE = "hr.xsd";
    public static final String HR_NAMESPACE =
        "http://www.binildas.com/apache/tuscany/sdo/sample";
    public CreateEmployees(Integer commentaryLevel) {
        super(commentaryLevel, SAMPLE_LEVEL_BASIC);
    }
    public static void main(String[] args) throws Exception{
        CreateEmployees sample =
            new CreateEmployees(COMMENTARY_FOR_NOVICE);
        sample.runSample();
    }
    public void runSample() throws Exception{

        HelperContext scope = createScopeForTypes();

        loadTypesFromXMLSchemaFile(scope, HR_XSD_RESOURCE);
        DataFactory factory = scope.getDataFactory();
        DataObject purchaseOrder = factory.create(HR_NAMESPACE,
            "employees");
        DataObject employee1 = purchaseOrder.createDataObject(
                            "employee");
        employee1.setString("id", "3457");
        employee1.set("name", "Cindy Jones");
        DataObject homeAddress1 = employee1.createDataObject("address");
        homeAddress1.set("street1", "Cindy Jones");
        homeAddress1.set("city", "Stanchion");
        homeAddress1.set("state", "TX");
        homeAddress1.set("zip-code", "79021");
        DataObject organization1 =
            employee1.createDataObject("organization");
        organization1.setString("id", "78");
        organization1.set("name", "Sales");
        DataObject office1 = employee1.createDataObject("office");
        office1.setString("id", "43");
        DataObject officeAddress1 = office1.createDataObject("address");
        officeAddress1.set("street1", "567 Murdock");
```

```
officeAddress1.set("street2", "Suite 543");
officeAddress1.set("city", "Millford");
officeAddress1.set("state", "TX");
officeAddress1.set("zip-code", "79025");
DataObject employee2 = purchaseOrder.createDataObject(
                        "employee");
employee2.setString("id", "30376");
employee2.set("name", "Linda Mendez");
DataObject homeAddress2 = employee1.createDataObject("address");
homeAddress2.set("street1", "423 Black Lake Road");
homeAddress2.set("street2", "Appartment 7A");
homeAddress2.set("city", "Boston");
homeAddress2.set("state", "MA");
homeAddress2.set("zip-code", "20967");
DataObject organization2 =
    employee2.createDataObject("organization");
organization2.setString("id", "78");
organization2.set("name", "HR");
DataObject office2 = employee2.createDataObject("office");
office2.setString("id", "48");
DataObject officeAddress2 = office2.createDataObject("address");
officeAddress2.set("street1", "5666 Cambridge Drive");
officeAddress2.set("city", "Boston");
officeAddress2.set("state", "MA");
officeAddress2.set("zip-code", "20968");

OutputStream stream = new FileOutputStream(HR_XML_RESOURCE_NEW);
scope.getXMLHelper().save(purchaseOrder, HR_NAMESPACE,
    "employees", stream);
stream.close();

XMLDocument doc =
    scope.getXMLHelper().createDocument(purchaseOrder,
    HR_NAMESPACE, "employees");
scope.getXMLHelper().save(doc, System.out, null);
System.out.println();
    }
}
```

Build and Run the SDO Sample

To build the sample in a single command, it is easy for you to go to `ch04\sdo` folder and execute the following command:

```
cd ch04\sdo
ant
```

Now, you can execute the `ReadEmployees` class by executing:

```
ant read
```

Now, you can execute the `CreateEmployees` class by executing:

```
ant create
```

Service Component Architecture

We have been creating IT assets in the form of programs and codes since many years, and been implementing SOA architecture. This doesn't mean that we follow a big bang approach and throw away all old assets in place of new. Instead, the success of any SOA effort depends largely on how we can make the existing assets co-exist with new architecture principles and patterns. To this end, **Service Component Architecture** (**SCA**) aims at creating new and transforms existing, IT assets into re-usable services more easily. These IT assets can then be rapidly adapted to changing business requirements. In this section, we will introduce SCA and also look into some working samples for the same.

What is SCA?

SCA introduces the notion of services and references. A component which implements some business logic offers their capabilities through service-oriented interfaces. Components may also consume functionality offered by other components through service-oriented interfaces, called service references. If you follow SOA best practices, you will perhaps appreciate the importance of fine-grained tight coupling and coarse-grained loose coupling between components. SCA composition aids recursive assembly of coarse-grained components out of fine-grained tightly coupled components. These coarse-grained components can even be recursively assembled to form higher levels of coarse-grained components. In SCA, a composite is a recursive assembly of fine-grained components. All these are shown in the SCA assembly model in the following screenshot:

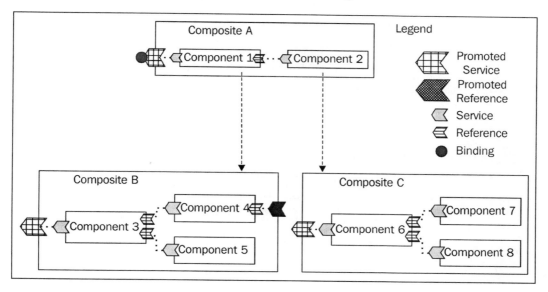

Apache Tuscany SCA Java

Apache Tuscany SCA is a sub-project within open-source Apache Tuscany, which has got a Java implementation of SCA. Tuscany SCA is integrated with Tomcat, Jetty, and Geronimo.

SCA Java runtime is composed of core and extensions. The core wires functional units together and provides SPIs that extensions can interact with. Extensions enhance SCA runtime functionality such as service discovery, reliability, support for transport protocols, and so on.

Tuscany SCA Java is available for download at: `http://incubator.apache.org/ tuscany/sca-java.html`.

SCA Sample Using Tuscany SCA Java

The sample here provides a single booking service with a default SCA (java) binding. The `BookingAgentServiceComponent` exercises this component by calling three other components that is, `FlightServiceComponent`, `HotelServiceComponent`, and `CabServiceComponent` as shown in the `BookingAgent` SCA assembly diagram shown below:

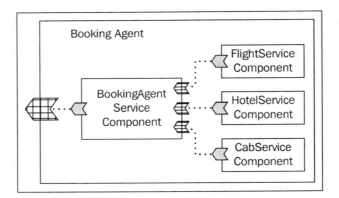

Code the Sample Artifacts

The sample consists of two sets of artifacts. The first set is the individual fine-grained service components. The second set is the coarse-grained service component, which wires the referenced fine-grained service components.

Code Fine-Grained Service Components

There are three fine-grained service components whose code is self explanatory and are listed below:

FlightServiceComponent

```
public interface IFlightService{
    String bookFlight(String date, int seats, String flightClass);
}
public class FlightServiceImpl implements IFlightService{
    public String bookFlight(String date, int seats, String
flightClass){
        System.out.println("FlightServiceImpl.bookFlight...");
        return "Success";
    }
}
```

HotelServiceComponent

```
public interface IHotelService{
    String bookHotel(String date, int beds, String hotelClass);
}
public class HotelServiceImpl implements IHotelService{
    public String bookHotel(String date, int beds, String hotelClass){
        System.out.println("HotelServiceImpl.bookHotel...");
        return "Success";
    }
}
```

CabServiceComponent

```
public interface ICabService{
    String bookCab(String date, String cabType);
}
public class CabServiceImpl implements ICabService{
    public String bookCab(String date, String cabType){
        System.out.println("CabServiceImpl.bookCab...");
        return "Success";
    }
}
```

Code BookingAgent Service Component

BookingAgentServiceComponent depends on three referenced service components, which are the fine-grained service components listed previously. They are initialized by the dependency injection by the SCA runtime. Also, for the actual business method invocation, the call is delegated to the referenced service components as shown in the bookTourPackage method in the following code:

```
import org.osoa.sca.annotations.Reference;
public class BookingAgentServiceComponent implements IBookingAgent{
    private IFlightService flightService;
    private IHotelService hotelService;
    private ICabService cabService;
    @Reference
    public void setFlightService(IFlightService flightService) {
        this.flightService = flightService;
    }
    @Reference
    public void setHotelService(IHotelService hotelService) {
        this.hotelService = hotelService;
    }
    @Reference
    public void setCabService(ICabService cabService) {
        this.cabService = cabService;
    }
    public String bookTourPackage(String date,
            int people, String tourPack){
        System.out.println("BookingAgent.bookTourPackage...");
        String flightBooked =
            flightService.bookFlight(date, people, tourPack);
        String hotelBooked =
            hotelService.bookHotel(date, people, tourPack);
        String cabBooked = cabService.bookCab(date, tourPack);
        if((flightBooked.equals("Success")) &&
                (hotelBooked.equals("Success")) &&
                (cabBooked.equals("Success"))){
            return "Success";
        }
        else{
            return "Failure";
        }
    }
}
```

Code BookingAgent Client

The BookingAgentClient first creates an instance of SCADomain and then gets a reference of the BookingAgentServiceComponent using the name of the configured service component. Then it executes the business method, bookTourPackage.

```
import org.apache.tuscany.sca.host.embedded.SCADomain;
public class BookingAgentClient{
    public static void main(String[] args) throws Exception {
        SCADomain scaDomain =
            SCADomain.newInstance("BookingAgent.composite");
        IBookingAgent bookingAgent =
            scaDomain.getService(IBookingAgent.class,
                "BookingAgentServiceComponent");
        System.out.println("BookingAgentClient.bookingTourPackage...");
        String result = bookingAgent.bookTourPackage(
            "20Dec2008", 5, "Economy");
        System.out.println("BookingAgentClient.bookedTourPackage : "
            + result);
        scaDomain.close();
    }
}
```

Build and Run the SCA Sample

To build the sample in a single command, it is easy for you to go to ch04\sca folder and execute the following command:

```
cd ch04\sca
ant
```

Now, you can execute the BookingAgentClient program by executing:

```
ant run
```

You can see that the `BookingAgentServiceComponent` will delegates calls to book individual line items to the referred service components and if all the individual bookings are done right, the overall transaction is "success". The following figure shows the screenshot of such a success scenario:

```
Command Prompt                                               _ □ ×

D:\binil\com\java\com\binildas\mytextbooks\soaandjava\3216_0
4_Code\ch04\sca>ant run
Buildfile: build.xml

run:
    [java] BookingAgentClient.bookingTourPackage...
    [java] BookingAgentServiceComponent.bookTourPackage...
    [java] FlightServiceImpl.bookFlight...
    [java] HotelServiceImpl.bookHotel...
    [java] CabServiceImpl.bookCab...
    [java] BookingAgentClient.bookedTourPackage : Success

BUILD SUCCESSFUL
Total time: 3 seconds
D:\binil\com\java\com\binildas\mytextbooks\soaandjava\3216_0
4_Code\ch04\sca>
```

Message-Oriented Middleware

Having seen some of the newer technology approaches in integrating data and services, we now need to move on to the next stage of discussion on the different platform level services available for integration. **message-oriented middleware (MOM)** is the main aspect we need to discuss in this context.

What is MOM?

Just like using sockets for **Inter-Process Communications (IPC)**, we use messaging when multiple processes need to communicate with each other to share data. Of course we can get the same effect when we use files or use a shared database for data level integration. But at times we may also require other **Quality of service (QoS)** features, a few amongst them will be described later. Thus, a MOM manages the movement of messages between systems connected by a network in a reliable fashion by separating the message sending step from the message receiving step so that the message exchange takes place in a loosely coupled and detached manner. The dynamics of message delivery in a MOM is shown in the following figure:

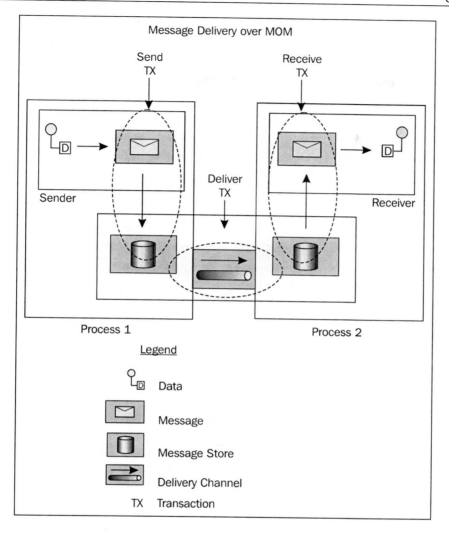

Here, the message delivery happens in the following steps:

- The sender process will just 'fire and forget' the message.
- The MOM will 'store and forward' the message.
- The receiver process will 'asynchronously receive' the message later.

Since the entire process happens in stages, even if one of the players in one of these stages is not ready for the message transmission, it won't affect the previous stages or the players involved there.

Benefits of Using MOM

MOM will have a set of features which makes it different from other style of communications such as RPC or Sockets, which may be required by some class of applications. Let us now look into some of these features.

- **Asynchronous Style of communication**: In MOM communications, a sender application after sending the message need not wait for either the sending of the message to complete or to get a response from the receiving applications. Both these after effects can be affected later, perhaps in a different thread of execution. This will increase application responsiveness.

- **Platform or Language level interoperability**: The world is never ideal, and we never have the luxury to always work with cutting edge technologies alone or to chose the platform or language of choice of all interconnecting systems. Sometimes there may be legacy systems, while sometimes there may be SOA-based web service interfaces to interconnect. Whatever be the case, a MOM allows them all to communicate through a common messaging paradigm. This universal connectivity is sometimes called as the Message Bus pattern.

- **Application down times**: Applications interconnecting together can sit in any geography or in any time zone, and all of them will have their own down times too. Hence, if a sender application sends some message to a receiver and the receiving application is not up at that time, the message shouldn't get lost. Further, when the receiver comes up the next time, it should receive the message once and exactly once. An MOM, with it's store and forward capability will give the maximum flexibility for interacting systems to exchange messages at their own pace.

- **Peak time processing and Throttling**: For a receiving application, there may be peak hours of the day during which it cannot process further request messages. Any further processing might degrade even the undergoing request processing. Hence, some kind of admission control or queuing up of additional requests to be processed further is required. Such mechanisms are the norm for a MOM with its store queues.

- **Reliability**: Message stores are introduced at multiple stages in the message delivery path. At the sender's end and at the receiver's end, message stores will guarantee staged message delivery which guarantees message reliability in stages. So, if a step in the message delivery fails, the step can be replayed retrieving the message again from the previous step (or previous stage message store).

- **Mediating services**: By using a MOM, an application becomes disconnected from the other applications. One application needs to reconnect only to the messaging system, not to all the other messaging applications it need to interconnect with. The applications are thus loosely coupled, still interconnected.

All the above features distinguish MOM from its counterpart styles of message interactions, which we leverage in many architectural patterns such as the Enterprise Service Bus, which we shall describe next.

Enterprise Service Bus

Enterprise Service Bus (ESB) is an architectural style for integrating systems, applications, and services. ESB provides a technology stack which acts like an integration bus to which multiple applications can talk. So, if two or more applications need to talk to each other, they don't need to integrate directly, but only need to talk to the ESB. The ESB will do the mediation services on behalf of the communicating applications, which may or may not be transparent to these communicating applications.

EAI and ESB

In order to understand ESB better, we need to understand the technical context under which we have to discuss this concept. The context is **Enterprise Application Integration (EAI)**, which deals with the sharing of data and processes, amongst connected systems in an enterprise. Traditionally, we have been doing EAI to do integration. EAI defines connection points between systems and applications. But when we consider integration in the context of SOA, we need to think more than just integration—we need to think in terms of services and service-based integration. Services expose standards, and if there is a way to leverage this standardization in services in defining the integration points too, then it would open up new possibilities in terms of standard connectors and adaptors.

Before we get into the details of ESB, it makes sense to compare and contrast it with other integration architectures as well. In EAI, the Point-to-Point, and the Hub and Spoke architectures are frequently used in many bespoke solutions. They are used in many vendor products too. These architectures are schematically shown in the following figure:

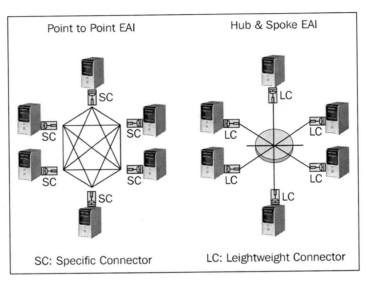

In Point-to-point, we define an integration solution for a pair of applications. At the integration points, we have tight coupling, since both ends have knowledge about their peers. Each peer combination need to have its own set of connectors. Hence, the number of connectors increases as the number of applications increases. Whereas in the Hub and Spoke architecture, we have a centralized hub (or broker) to which all applications are connected. Each application connects with the central hub through lightweight connectors. The lightweight connectors facilitates for application integration with minimum or zero changes to the existing applications.

Now, we will look into the Enterprise Message Bus and the Enterprise Service
Bus architectures.

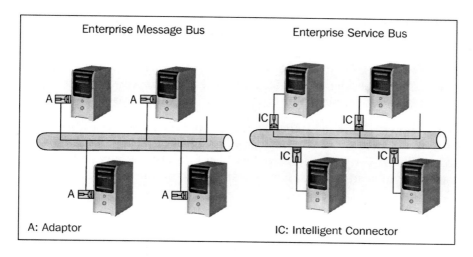

The Enterprise Message Bus makes use of the MOM stack and toolset to provide
a common messaging backbone for applications to interconnect. Sometimes, the
applications have to use adapter which handles scenarios such as invoking CICS
transactions. Such an adapter may provide connectivity between the applications
and the message bus using proprietary bus APIs, and application APIs.

When you move from a traditional MOM to the ESB-based architecture, the major
difference is that the applications communicate through a **Service Oriented
Architecture (SOA)** backbone. This backbone is again built over the common MOM,
but it provides Intelligent Connectors. These Intelligent Connectors are abstract in
the sense that they only define the transport binding protocols and service interface,
not the real implementation details. They are intelligent, because they have logic
built-in along with the ESB to selectively bind to services at run time. This capability
enhances agility for applications by allowing late binding of services and deferred
service choice. Moreover, since these intelligent connectors are deployable in the ESB
runtime, they are even available as **COTS (component off the shelf)** libraries. This
means that the ESB will open up a market for vendors to build and sell connectors
for proprietary EIS systems, which will expose standard interfaces outside the ESB.

Java Business Integration

Java Business Integration (JBI) provides a collaboration framework which provides standard interfaces for integration components and protocols to plug into, thus allowing the assembly of **Service Oriented Integration (SOI)** frameworks following the ESB pattern. JBI is based on JSR 208, which is an extension of Java 2 Enterprise Edition (J2EE) and is specific for JBI **Service Provider Interfaces (SPI)**. SOA and SOI are the targets of JBI and hence it is built around WSDL. Integration components can be plugged into the JBI environment using a service model-based on WSDL.

For readers who would like to delve deep into Java Business Integration, you are advised to refer to *"Service Oriented Java Business Integration"* by Binildas A. Christudas ISBN: 1847194400 published by Packt Publishing, since we cannot cover such a vast topic in a single section or in a single chapter in a book.

OpenESB

Project OpenESB is an open-source implementation of JSR-208 (JBI) hosted by Java. net community and is available for download at `https://open-esb.dev.java. net/`. OpenESB allows easy integration of web services thus creating loosely coupled enterprise class composite applications.

OpenESB Architecture provides the following salient features, which distinguishes itself from other closed ESB solutions available in the market today:

- **Application Server support**: OpenESB has got good integration with Glassfish application server, thus enabling the integration components to leverage the reliability, scalability, resiliency, deployment, and management capabilities of the application server.

- **Composite application support**: In OpenESB, we can use BPEL and similar composite application support tools to create composite applications which are self-contained artifacts that contain other sub-artifacts.

- **Composite Application Editor**: OpenESB comes with Composite Application Editor that helps the user 'wire-together' and create new Composite Applications from fine-grained services.

- **JBI Bus**: The JBI Bus provides a pluggable infrastructure which can host a set of integration component, which can integrate various types of IT assets in the enterprise. The JBI bus provides an in-memory messaging bus called the **Normalized Message Router (NMR)**. It is through this NMR the messages which are normalized and in standard abstract WSDL format flows.

- **Service Engines and Binding Components**: JBI supports two types of components, such as Service Engines and Binding Components. Service Engines provide business logic and transformation services to other components, as well as consume such services. Binding components provide services external to the OpenESB environment available to the NMR.

- **Business Logic Units**: These are processing units similar to a BPEL component which can orchestrate the services available at the ESB and provide higher level of business process functionality again at the ESB.

- **Global Service Collaboration Networks**: OpenESB supports for a services fabric style of service assembly which is a kind of service virtualization which divides the organization's information assets into "Virtual Services" without regard to the transport or binding protocol of the actual implementation components.

- **Monitoring**: OpenESB also provides the ability to centrally monitor, manage, and administer the distributed runtime system of the ESB.

Another noticeable factor which advocates the popularity of OpenESB is the huge list of components and library support available in the industry which can plug easily into the OpenESB JBI infrastructure, a part of which is shown in the following screenshot taken from the OpenESB website:

By Function	By Solution	By Name
Application Mashup AOSD Aspects Aspect SE Communications These components provide different methods of communicating with other components of the Enterprise Service Bus. ADABAS Natural CICS BC CORBA BC DCOM BC File BC FTP BC HL7 BC HTTP BC SIP BC UDDI BC XMPP BC Data Conversion Translating different data formats among systems with varying requirements. ETL SE XSLT SE Data Extraction and Transformation ETL SE SQL SE Data Integration ETL SE Data Mashup Database Connection Components that allow connection and inspection of databases. Informix JMS BC JDBC BC Oracle SAP Sybase Event Processing IEP SE Java EE SQL SE Orchestration and Collaboration BPEL SE	Healthcare These components provide solutions for the healthcare industry. HL7 BC Mainframe These components provide mainframe solutions to integration. CICS BC IMS BC Telecommunications These components provide solutions for the telecommunications industry. CORBA BC SIP BC SNMP BC XMPP BC	Alphabetical Listing If you know the name of the project you are looking for, find it here. Applications Mural Binding Components CICS BC CORBA BC DCOM BC eMail BC File BC FTP BC HL7 BC HTTP BC JMS BC JDBC BC JMS BC LDAP BC MQ Series BC MSMQ BC RSS BC SAP BC SIP BC SMTP BC SNMP BC SWIFT BC TCPIP BC UDDI BC XMPP BC Service Engines Aspect SE BPEL SE Data Mashup Encoding SE ETL SE IEP SE Scripting SE SQL SE WLM SE XSLT SE

Summary

SOA is not a single product or single reference architecture to be followed, but is all about best practices, reference architectures, processes, toolsets, and frameworks along with many other things which will help you and your organization increase the responsiveness and agility of your enterprise architecture. Standards and frameworks play a greater role in enabling easy and widespread industry adoption of SOA. In this chapter, you have seen few emerging standards such as SDO and SCA, addressing from data integration till service and component integration. Newer architectural patterns such as ESB and Data Services provide you with a wider framework upon which you can enable your integration points for open and flexible information flow. In the next chapter, we will specifically look more into integration with emphasis on these new architectural styles and patterns.

5

Traditional Integration Technology

In this chapter, we will look into a couple of case studies, of which, the solutions for one of the cases is based on the principles of EAI, while in the other, the solution is based on SOA fundamentals.

In the concluding part of the case study based on EAI, we will look into the drawbacks of EAI that we can overcome by using solution based on SOA.

Case Study #1—Based on EAI

Customer Information

The client is a major FMCG industry with stores and warehouses all over the country. It sells various brands and serves millions of customers in a financial year. The company has a mix of modern technology and legacy application that has been serving its need over several years.

Business Need

The typical business model of the client is supply chain management. They ran the business based on various in-house CRM and e-commerce monolithic solutions. But the need to integrate the systems arose when the company started growing, and it had various business partners. The business partners had to be integrated with the business processes of that internal system, which until now were operating as independent software solutions.

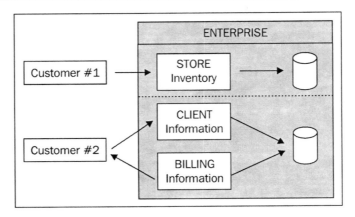

As we can see in the preceding figure, the internal processes of the enterprise run independent of each other. The software that runs for each of these units of work is less automated and needs a lot of manual intervention. Any change in the data at stores has to be manually fed again at the shop floor for billing the customer purchases. Also, some of the deployed solution had to be duplicated in each of the systems to achieve identical results.

The core business needs of the client were:

- Integration between internal business processes and business partners
- Avoiding duplicity
- Achieving re-usability, flexibility, and scalability
- Platform independence
- Setting up messaging exchange
- Reducing manual intervention
- Cost effectiveness

Solution

Before diving into the solution, we will talk a bit about EAI. We would take up each of the term separately that is E, A, and I.

"E" in EAI is for **Enterprise**. Enterprise is analogous to an organization, which constitutes different departments to achieve some business goal. To achieve a business goal, the department will focus on delivering it based on fewer efforts, lower costs, reusability, and so on.

So here the "A", that is **Application**, comes into the picture. Departments use various applications to get the product delivery-based on the above criteria. Say the purchase department uses an application to keep track of the product inventory. But then the purchase department also has to communicate with the sales department to keep track of the products sold, so that whenever the re-order level of a product is reached, they can go ahead. How will that be done?

Now, we shall talk about the "I" that is **Integration**. The applications between the departments have to be integrated so that the information can be exchanged whenever and wherever necessary.

We have tried to explain EAI, in one of the simplest forms. EAI in a nutshell would be helpful in:

- Communicating between two or more applications to fulfill a business goal.
- Reducing cost and turnaround time, thereby increasing productivity.
- Streamlining business process to achieve greater customer satisfaction.

As a solution for our organization, each of these heterogeneous systems had to communicate and exchange messages. To do that, they had to be integrated. So it was decided to implement the solution in the 'hub and spoke' architecture.

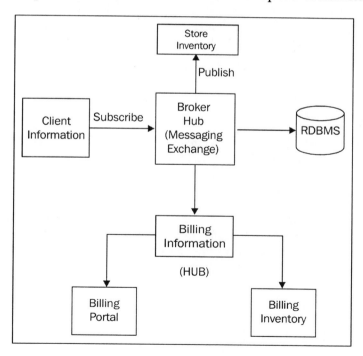

Hub and Spoke Architecture

This is a fine example of a centralized architecture. In a system designed in a 'hub and spoke architecture', the hub acts as a centralized messaging server. Applications act as spokes and are tied to the hub. Communication between each of the application is through the hub. The important point to note is that, though an application is tied to the hub, it can also act as a hub to other systems. This is shown in the preceding image.

Designing the solution in a 'hub and spoke' architecture will be helpful for:

- Message flow, as the hub acts as a server and all messages will pass through it.
- Communication pattern will be Publish-Server and Server-Subscribe.
- All the messages queued up in the server and also to minimize loss of message in case the subscribing application is down.

So, the organization started its efforts towards re-aligning the systems and application according to EAI standards.

Step One—Identifying Applications (Spokes)

Not all organizations have the same type of applications. A certain number of baseline business needs have to be determined so that a choice can be made as to which of the business processes need to be optimized. They can be based on:

1. Number of transactions
2. Number of data interchange protocols
3. Type of application

Applications are determined based on the above parameters—the number of transactions handled will be quite helpful for capacity planning for that node. Conditional values are set in the hub to handle a certain number of transactions and setup alert messages in case of inconsistent performance.

Another important parameter is the protocol. It is here where we define the manner in which the data can be interchanged. For example, a certain system or application would be either sending or receiving information through HTTP or SMTP. So the exchange protocol is either HTTP or SMTP.

The third important parameter is the type of application that needs to be part of integration. The application type would determine the method of communication, for example, the type of adapter that could be used. As an example, the application could be custom software that would help the sales department keep track of the inventory, or it could be a part of the SAP implementation taken up by the organization recently. So here we can either choose a custom SAP adapter, or make a choice of another adapter that can take information from this application.

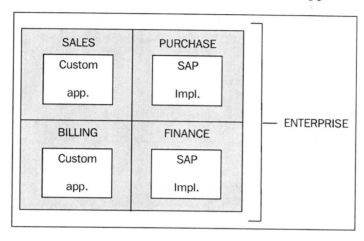

The list of applications that might be the part of the integration framework is now determined and documented. As soon as we have the list of applications, we prod further into each of these applications. Here, we will start determining the schema that shall be required for the data to be exchanged. All the variable data types and sizes are listed.

The second part shall contain relationship information for the database it interacts or it might be connected to any other application for pre or post processing.

All the information is thus documented so that it can be of immense help while building the framework.

Step Two—Messaging Hub

As a second step, we had to set up a messaging hub. The hub will help in the exchange of information with the right set of applications. Proprietary message broker tool was identified that would enable applications to publish and subscribe messages. The message broker acts as a messaging hub. This hub will receive information from the application that would either have to be published to a particular application, or broadcast to all applications depending upon the set-up rules. The hub would be helpful for:

Transfer Information: The moment a piece of information, that is document(s), is received by the hub, the content is studied in accordance with the schema. It will check for the sender information and the receiver information. Once the details are processed, the hub will pass the document to the receiver. In this scenario, each of the documents will have the sender and receiver information.

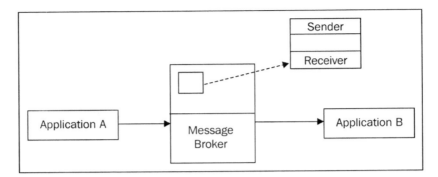

Document Repository and Registry: As soon as any document is received at the hub, the information is stored in the database. The database will have information about the sender, receiver, time of delivery, status of delivery, and other such information. This information helps in keeping track of the document processing.

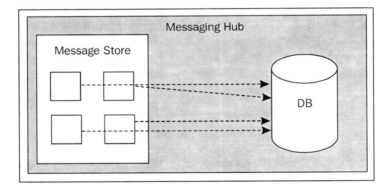

Process Management: Rules are set up to relay alerts, in case, a document processing fails. This helps the organization manage processes in case of failures, and thereby prevent losses, and take proactive measures to pre-empt recurrence. It can also help in real-time monitoring of the flow of documents between the systems.

Rules Engine: For each of the messages flowing across the hub, rules are set up for delivery and storage of the messages. The document delivery could be set up and storage can either be volatile or guaranteed. Depending on the storage type, the hub will store the document in-memory (or in-memory and on disk). Based on a business activity, notifications are set up for information to be fetched and delivered. For example, let us say an 'Insert Notification' is set up on the sales table in the database. So as soon as a row is inserted in the sales table, a notification will pick up the required information and will pass it across to the other applications based on integration setup.

Management Services: The hub setup is done using a UI provided by the broker toolset. The main services provided by the UI are setting up of documents, rules, and notifications. It can also be used to keep track of the document exchange. The Publish-Subscribe values for the document can be tracked using the UI.

So the hub was set up for:

1. Integrating applications
2. Integrating database
3. Document or Information Exchange
4. Protocol setup

This brings us to the crux of the matter, how will the information from different systems be exchanged. How will the information from an application sending XML document be converted to database understandable values? Well, that is explained in the next step.

Step Three—Identifying Adapter

The core medium for communication to any integration framework is through adapters. It is through adapters that information is being exchanged between the integrated applications, the spokes and the hub. The underlying mechanism adopted by adapters varies with the provider. But basically, they help in transformation of the information from documents into target understandable values.

Each of the adapters has sets of instructions that are hidden from the end users, but which help in the exchange of information. The popular adapters are file adapters, database adapters (for example, JDBC Adapters), and application adapters (for example, SAP adapters). These adapters help to parse files, or get data from SAP adapters, or execute database services. Choice of the adapter usually depends on the type of source and the target.

In our case, for database actions, we have used JDBC Adapters. The services offered by the adapter help in:

1. Executing database actions of Insert, Update, and Delete
2. Setting up connection pools for connections re-use
3. Transformation of information that is, mapping decimal values to float data type, and mapping date and time formats

SAP adapters were used for getting data from SAP implementation and integrating it to the database. Similarly, from custom applications, data was published as flat files and using flat file adapters, they were synced to the backend database tables. Also, data between the custom application and SAP implementations were exchanged using flat file and SAP adapters.

It would be needful to say that configuring these adapters with the applications and the hub does require a fair bit of programming. The programming takes care of handling the events and notifications. Also, various transformation services need to be called to process data. Those services could either be built-in, or programmatically created in case of a custom requirement. For huge applications, there could be loads of mappings between variables. This is required to process the data in the target understandable format.

When all the above steps are followed, the integration solution is set up. Voila!! Your enterprise application integration solution is ready.

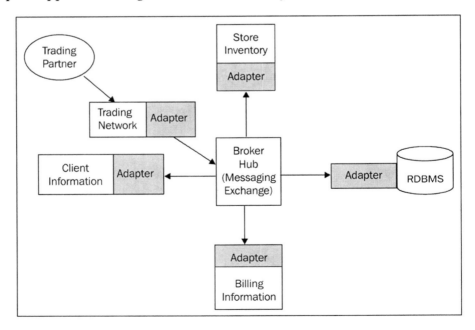

The preceding image depicts integration between various systems in an enterprise. Now, we can see that the systems, which were hitherto monolithic, can communicate with each other. Also, external systems, say trading partners, communicate to the message broker using 'Trading Network' setups and adapters.

Goals Achieved

With the re-organization of systems and the improvements in system design, excellent results started flowing in. It helped in improved performance of business transactions, efficient coordination, and productivity. This made the organization achieve the goals that were initially set initially while designing the solution.

Goal #1—Integration between Internal Business Processes and Business Partners

This was achieved using the 'hub and spoke' model, where the business processes and partners interacted through the hub. The individual silos of systems were able to communicate with each other using the hub.

Goal #2—Avoid Duplicity

With the applications communicating with each other, and a centralization of the database, the duplicity of data was avoided to a great extent. Also, the need for handling multiple transactions was eliminated because of the choice of two-phased commits.

Goal #3—Achieve Re-Usability, Flexibility, and Scalability

We achieved asset re-usability by having the integration services designed in a way that it can perform multiple roles, for example, the file transfer service. Given different parameters, the same service can transfer files across multiple systems. These also helped in having a flexible approach to the system design, as the assets could be moved, added, or phased out. So the new system was scalable in terms of performance. It could handle multiple transactions, and had the capability of parallel processing of transactions.

On the document level, the same was achieved using the semantic mappings of each attribute. So data from the source was easily converted to the target understandable formats.

Goal #4—Platform Independence

The proprietary integration server could be installed and run on different OS. Saying this, the spokes, that is the systems that were integrated, could run on any of the platforms. The hub or the integration server was unaware of the target systems platform, and all the communication between the source and the target was done either through the standard adapter, or through the customized version of the adapter. So, we could do away with the problems of the underlying platforms.

Goal #5—Setting up Messaging Exchange

The integration server is the core messaging hub for the system. All the messages between the systems are routed through the hub. The standard message exchange protocol is through SOAP or SMTP. To minimize the loss of message, the exchange can be set-up to have a guaranteed delivery mechanism. This way, in case the target system is down, the message gets queued up, and as soon as the target system comes up, the message gets delivered.

Goal #6—Less Manual Intervention

Within the new design, the systems communicate with each other through the hub. This gives us the flexibility to automate more business processes and add to the integration world. The business processing could be purchase order processing, wherein once the re-order level of an item is reached at the warehouse, the business process would automatically raise a purchase request and send it to the business partner. The manual intervention to check the re-order level, raising the purchase request, and then mailing it to the partner is totally eliminated.

Goal #7—Cost Effective

Until the solution was implemented, the information between the disparate systems was exchanged either manually, or by undergoing several pre- and post-processing rules. Dependencies were hard to eliminate, and improving business was a challenge. With the implementation of this solution, the turnaround time for the execution of orders improved considerably thereby reducing overheads effectively. This in turn made the business cost-effective.

EAI Drawbacks

The successful implementation of the new design did have its own share of challenges. These challenges can be broadly categorized as follows:

Proprietary Architecture

As we have seen earlier, most of the integration between the systems is done through the proprietary adapters.

Messaging Bottlenecks

As we have seen, the message exchange between the systems is always through the Hub. This creates a lot of maintenance issues for the hub. When the systems grow bigger, and the number of transactions between the systems increases, the flow of message grows tremendously, and a message bottleneck is reached. This could crash the hub, leading to high expenses towards setting up a failover mechanism and retrieving the lost messages. Moreover, much business is also lost.

Tight Coupling

Businesses are tied to each other through hubs and adapters. This creates a one-way communication channel between the systems. Also, the strict mapping with the hub will result in a tight coupling between the applications and the hub. Otherwise, without the hub and the adapter, none of the systems can communicate with each other.

Non-Flexible Architecture

Due to the tight coupling between the applications, a lot of dynamics would have to be taken care of, when any new system is added. That would range between investing on better integration server (hub), investing in adapter services, addition of manpower, and also change in architecture, to involve the new system.

Manpower

The final, but among the most critical, hazards of an EAI-based approach is getting experienced manpower, including a rare breed of architects, developers, and testers. Developing a solution based on EAI requires expertise in different technical aspects. Also, because they are proprietary tools, training requires a good amount of investment.

SOA to Rescue

With more systems being added to the framework, the cost of maintenance had been increasing gradually. To overcome these drawbacks, it was decided to move the integration framework to a more flexible unit. In the subsequent part, we will explain why SOA became the popular choice.

In the earlier chapters, we have already seen what SOA is. So we won't look into it again except to give a little foreword in case you are just looking at this chapter.

Let us emphasize once again on one particular statement– *SOA is not a solution, it is a practice*. You really cannot put it under the category of a solution. It is a practice which has to be implemented by each of the stakeholders in an enterprise. It is really not easy to change the perception, but to seek out the maximum benefit out of an SOA-based practice, a lot more groundwork has to be done. Firstly, the core of the term has to be understood. Merely stating that it is a solution based on web service will not qualify it to become an SOA-based approach.

In Chapter 4, we have categorically explained the terms, "services", "orientation", and "architecture". As we did with EAI, we have to go into the details of each of these terms. To put it briefly, we convert the business processes to "services", and expose it to be "oriented" with its business goal. The software design "architecture" that conforms to this is SOA.

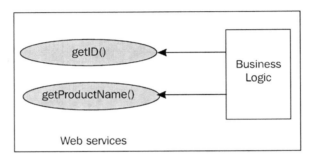

As we have seen above, two web services have been carved out from one of the sets of business logic. The web services are an interface for the outside world, whereas the dynamics of business is hidden inside the 'Business Logic'.

The three conceptual units that constitute an SOA-based solution are:

- Service Provider (Service)
- Service Consumer (Consumer)
- Directory Services (enabled by Broker)

You can see them in the following diagram, which explains the basic properties of SOA:

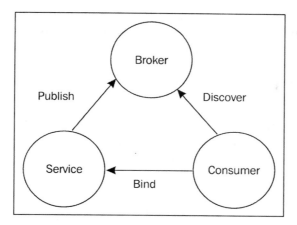

We will try to base our solution on the principles stated earlier.

Case Study #2—Based on SOA

Now for the current scenario, we would like to design a solution based on SOA instead of using proprietary EAI tool. The foremost need for the organization was to break-up its current IT infrastructure. The departments had to be broken up further based on the functionalities of each business unit. The business units had legacy applications, monolithic software units, or a partially networked solution.

The main aspect of having a solution on SOA is:

- Ease of use
- Easily portable
- Easily deployable
- Easily scalable

At the end of the case study, we will try to analyze our solution and see how successfully it has been implemented against each of the above aspects. As in the earlier case study, we will try to break the solution designed here into a few steps.

Step One—Defining Organization Assets

For the sake of designing solutions based on the tenets of SOA, we have to define each of the organization assets, which are the different business functions of the organization. These functions could be either a single process, or set of processes that effectively help in achieving a business goal. The assets have to be very specific in their definition, as one of the goals of SOA is about re-use of the assets. Each of the assets would belong to a set of libraries that are part of a searchable registry of services.

Also, the composite applications that are relevant to the execution of business logic have to be identified. The success of the solution depends on how these applications are designed to be scalable. The application could be made up of underlying business logic, and a front-end that hides the execution logic from the users.

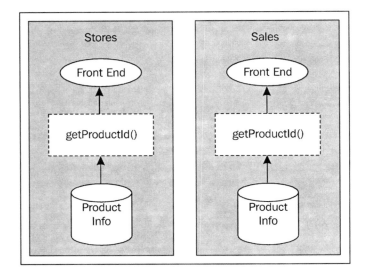

While considering a business function or sets of business functions to be an asset, we clearly need to have an idea about the following factors:

- Detailed business process
- Volume of transactions
- Dependencies on other assets

The business process was clearly detailed and documented. This was one basic tenet of the entire solution, as each of the business process had to be known.

We had to have an idea of the volume, a particular asset. The reason for the same was to have a clear understanding of the operational performance issue that we might have to face in the production environments, and a plan of action to mitigate such issues.

The third foremost factor was the dependencies of each of the assets, as we know that for achieving a business goal, various business processes have to be involved. These processes may span over multiple assets. So, each of these dependencies were documented for referencing while the services were being developed.

Step Two—Generate Services

Moving further, we need to define services out of the assets. Services are the mode of communication with the other assets that might have the need to consume the output of that service for further processing. In our opinion, for the creation of the service, it has to undergo a few sets of rules.

For the first one, we need to have a clear definition of the business goal that needs to be achieved. It has to be thought about quite clearly along with the list of dependencies. Once that is done, the services need to be created. These services would keep the business logic encapsulated. Then, it's time to deploy the services.

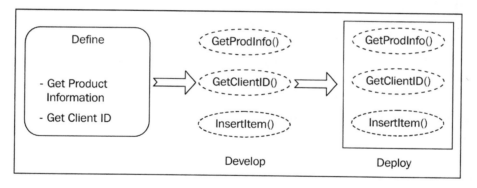

For the sake of preparing the design document for the entire solutions, each of the assets was clearly identified, and so were the services that were associated with the list of dependencies. Typically, each of the services are designed in such a way that they could be re-used by other applications. Designing the services in such a way made them 'interoperable', because it enabled them to communicate with other services without looking at the backend business logic, the platform in which they were developed, or the execution language.

The services designed here were granular in nature, in the sense that each of the services was typically carved out from the business functions. But, how will these services communicate? There are few different ways to communicate as we have seen in the earlier chapters. So, without digging into them, we chose one of the best approaches.

We chose XML — eXtensible Markup Language as the messaging format between each of the business functions. We have listed the advantages of XML in the earlier chapter. We will recap it here briefly. The advantages of XML are:

Information is eXtensible

'Extensible' is the USP for an XML. The popularity of XML owes itself to the demand of the industry to add on data into the current representation. This helps the developers to re-use the current form of representation and save the development time for the creation of additional data formats.

As tags represent each of the data functions, more tags could be added and information can be handled with greater thrust on re-use.

```
<Departments>
    <department>
        <name>Purchase</name>
        <location>IL</location>
        ...
    </departments>
    ...
</Departments>
```

Now, in a real-life scenario, let's say the organization goes across the border and sets up a 'purchase' department.

```
<Departments>
    <department>
        <name>Purchase</name>
        <country>United Kingdom</country>
        <location>London</location>
        ...
    </departments>
    ...
</Departments>
```

Information Represented in Textual Form

The information to be exchanged is stored in a textual format instead of in any binary forms of data. This makes it easily readable and understandable.

```
<Departments>
    <department>
        <name>Purchase</name>
        <location>IL</location>
        …..
    </departments>
    …..
</Departments>
```

As we noted in the listing above, the information is easily understandable in a way. It can be easily deduced whether the information, if belonging to the 'purchase' department, is located in 'IL'.

Information is Structured

The information stored within the XML is represented in a structured manner. From the above listing, we can see that the information is properly nested, and when any new department is to be listed, it can be easily represented. Also, if the 'purchase' department is started at any other location, the same can be represented in the schema.

Platform Independency

Due to its textual form of representation, the information in an XML format can be easily consumed by different technologies.

We will proceed further after representing the information in one of the most common forms of information exchange. Now, the services that have been created have to be identified by the consumers. How do we do that?

We decided to take the help of **WSDL (Web Services Description Language)** for the purpose of identifying the public interface of the web service. WSDL gives the ability to:

- Locate services
- Identify functions
- Bind messages

Typically a WSDL is represented in the following form:

```xml
<?xml version="1.0" encoding="UTF-8"?>
<definitions name="ProductService"
    targetNamespace="http://www.criorg.com/wsdl/ProductService.wsdl"
    xmlns="http://schemas.xmlsoap.org/wsdl/"
    xmlns:soap="http://schemas.xmlsoap.org/wsdl/soap/"
    xmlns:tns="http://www.criorg.com/wsdl/ProductService.wsdl"
    xmlns:xsd="http://www.w3.org/2001/XMLSchema">
    <message name="getProductName">
        <part name="prodName" type="xsd:string"/>
    </message>
    <message name="getProductId">
        <part name="prodId" type="xsd:int"/>
    </message>
    <portType name="Product_PortType">
        <operation name="getProduct">
            <input message="tns:getProductId"/>
            <output message="tns:getProductName"/>
        </operation>
    </portType>
    <binding name="Product_Binding" type="tns:Product_PortType">
        <soap:binding style="rpc"
            transport="http://schemas.xmlsoap.org/soap/http"/>
        <operation name="getProduct">
            <soap:operation soapAction=""/>
            <input>
                <soap:body
                    encodingStyle="http://schemas.xmlsoap.org/
                                soap/encoding/"
                    namespace="urn:examples:productservice"
                    use="encoded"/>
            </input>
            <output>
                <soap:body
                    encodingStyle="http://schemas.xmlsoap.org/
                                soap/encoding/"
                    namespace="urn:examples:productservice"
                    use="encoded"/>
            </output>
        </operation>
    </binding>
    <service name="Product_Service">
        <documentation>WSDL File for Product Service</documentation>
        <port binding="tns:Product_Binding" name="Product_Port">
            <soap:address
                location="http://localhost:8080/soap/servlet/rpcrouter"/>
        </port>
    </service>
</definitions>
```

The first part of the WSDL gives the definition of the schema, and other related elements. In the second part, messages are defined. The inputs and the outputs of the message along with the data type of each of them are presented. In the third part, the port-type are presented, based on the schema. It presents us with the list of operations that can be used for the particular web service. Then we have the binding type defined. This will give us the binding style and the manner in which the message would be transported. Finally, the endpoints will be shown. This will give us the location of the web service to be called.

In this WSDL, we are trying to retrieve the product information based on the product ID. We can generate similar WSDL for each of the business functions. The generation of the WSDL was an automated process for which we used the Cape Clear's SOA Editor toolkit.

Now that the WSDLs were generated, we had to design the transport mechanism for the services. In simple terms, the protocols had to be defined for the services to communicate. The bindings of the messages were decided on SOAP, which has the capacity to be transported over simple HTTP or TCP. It can even be transported via SMTP where asynchronous mode of messaging would be involved.

We will briefly look at the benefits of using SOAP:

- Protocol portability
- Capacity to generate WSDL and client classes automatically
- Ability to handle stateful conversation

The type of SOAP message that shall be used is defined in the WSDL:

```
...
<binding name="Product_Binding" type="tns:Product_PortType">
    <soap:binding style="rpc"
        transport="http://schemas.xmlsoap.org/soap/http"/>
....
```

The SOAP message was represented as:

```
<binding name="b1" type="tns:pt1">
    <operation name="GetProductInfo">
        <soap:operation soapAction=
                        "http://www.criorg.com/GetProductInfo"/>
            <input>
                <soap:body use="literal"/>
            </input>
            <output>
                <mime:multipartRelated>
                    <mime:part>
                        <soap:body parts="body"
```

```
                                              use="literal"/>
                      </mime:part>
                      <mime:part>
                          <mime:content part="docs"
                                         type="text/html"/>
                      </mime:part>
                      <mime:part>
                          <mime:content part="logo"
                                         type="image/gif"/>
                          <mime:content part="logo"
                                         type="image/jpeg"/>
                      </mime:part>
                  </mime:multipartRelated>
              </output>
      </operation>
  </binding>
  <service name="ProductInfoService">
      <port name="ProductInfoPort"binding="tns:b1">
          <soap:address location="http://www.criorg.com/productinfo"/>
      </port>
  </service>
```

Now, we have the entire services portfolio defined. The services part will generate the web services, its relevant WSDL, and define the transport mechanism.

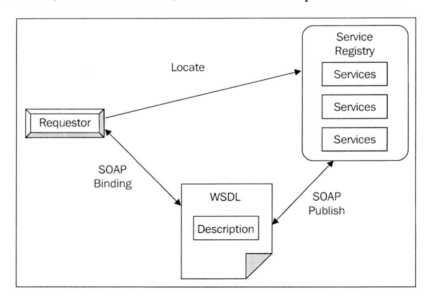

Step Three—Model

Once we had the service ready, we modeled the business processes of the organization to match the goals that were defined by the services. Each of the defined business processes was modeled.

We can use the several commercial design tools available to model the business processes. These models gave us the exact idea of the information flow between the systems. The model will encompass the following:

- Business Processes
- Relationships
- Protocols
- Service Providers
- Service Consumers

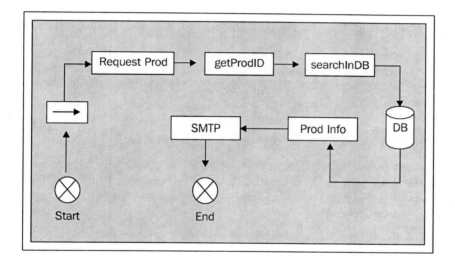

Shown in the preceding image is a typical business process that caters to the need of 'requesting product information'.

Process#1: Signals start of the process. This could be a trigger-based either on specific conditions, or it could be a scheduled job.

Process#2: This is the requestor of the business function for getting information on a product.

Process#3: This process will pass on a request to get the product with the product ID.

Process#4: This process will search in the database for the production information related to the product ID.

Process#5: The retrieved product information is wrapped in the messaging body.

Process#6: The message has to be sent to the consumer now. This is done using SMTP protocol.

Process#7: Once the process is complete, it will signal an 'End' to the processing of the model.

Proper design of a model is quite necessary, as it can help achieve the maximum value out of the flow of information from within an enterprise solution. So, the leveraging on integration of the services is deemed quite an important aspect for the solution to succeed.

The advantage of using the model-based approach is:

Co-relation of Events

The orchestration of each of the services is dependant on a particular event, or some set of events. When the model is designed, each of the event handlers is defined. This gives an idea about the processes that will be involved in case any of the events are triggered.

Co-relation of Services and Information

Information provided by any of the services could be consumed by a subsequent service, or any other endpoint. The model design takes care of representing the information within the services. This enables the users to check the state of information at any given time.

Step Four—Integrate

As soon as the business models were defined, we had to integrate those so that communication between the different business units could be possible. ESB is the core to the integration of those services.

ESB—Enterprise Service Bus

ESB is the communication backbone of any SOA-based solution. It plays a vital role in encompassing the solution, and is really the place through which the message exchange takes place. ESB supports:

Load Balancing: The tools that provide ESB service have special configuration segments that would deal with load balancing of the processes. The services could be deployed across multiple machines to achieve the same as well.

Transformation: The messages that are being processed consume and deliver objects of different data types. XML being the de-facto standard helps us to tune the information into the target understandable data type.

Message Portability: As we have seen, the provider of the data and the consumer will have no inkling about the underlying technologies. It could be a .NET service message being consumed by a service developed on Java, where even the OS don't matter.

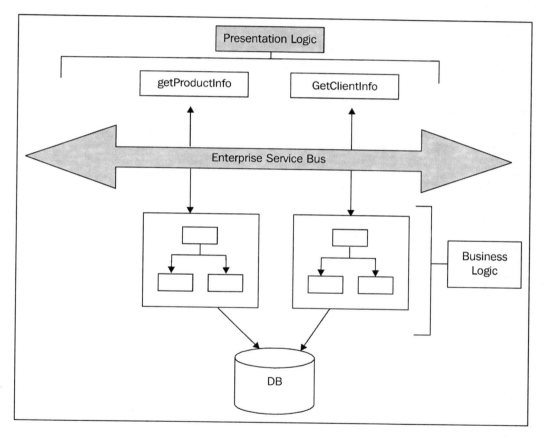

For the purpose of setting up an ESB, we decided to use 'OpenESB'. It is based upon **Java Business Integration (JBI)** specification. The open-source community develops OpenESB, and the NetBeans IDE supports it. Recently, the **OpenESB v2.0** was released as a preview version for the community. The new version allows the user the following capabilities:

- Loose Coupling
- Greater Inter-operability
- Greater Integration to other open-source services

This gives the users greater flexibility for development and deployment. It also helps in moving away from the proprietary use of ESB, and hence in conforming to the SOA standards of using less proprietary elements.

So now that we have the final solution ready, let's move ahead and analyze if the goals we set initially have been achieved.

Goals Achieved

Here, we will try to analyze the solution we implemented against the goals that had been set before embarking upon the journey to have a SOA solution.

Goal #1—Proprietary Architecture

By exposing the business functions as services, and through the maximum use of open-source toolsets, we eliminated the need to have a proprietary architecture. The consumers and producers being represented in BUS architecture act as a huge advantage against the standard hub-spoke model of development. Use of services also helped to move away from the proprietary adapter-based messaging.

Goal #2—Eliminating Messaging Bottlenecks

In the implementation of SOA solution, we shall be using the BUS as a medium of communication between the applications. The entire message flow is through the service bus. This gives the flexibility of load balancing and eliminates any messaging bottlenecks.

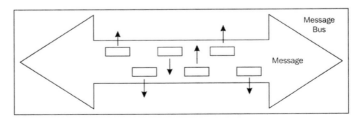

Goal #3—Loose Coupling of Applications

Due to the use of web services, the biggest gain in terms of portability is achieved. The messages can be propagated across multiple systems, and with the use of our friendly XML-based messaging, the dependency on the type of consumer application is lost. Today, most of the applications can consume XML data. This way, you can plug-in multiple systems and messages across the bus. This helps us to achieve loose coupling between the applications. 'N' number of systems could be added without affecting the current solution.

Goal #4—Flexible Architecture

A remarkable improvement in business is achieved by moving the messages across the bus system. Multiple applications can be plugged in for achieving the goals of integration. Also, with the use of WSDLs, we could do away with the configuration of adapters. This saves a lot of development time by re-using the WSDLs for future application message transactions.

Goal #5—Return On Investment (ROI)

With the maximum use of open-source application tools, benefits are seen on the organization's profit. Even when business grows, organizations need not set aside substantial amounts of money on infrastructure for maintaining proprietary solutions. The cost of manpower training also reduces.

The cascading effect of all those is felt on the development of the solutions. It helps organizations reduce their time to market, and helps them achieve customer satisfaction.

In brief, developing a SOA-based solution helped us achieve:

- Integration between internal business processes and business partners
- Avoidance of duplicity
- Re-usability, flexibility, and scalability
- Platform independence
- Improvement in messaging exchange performance
- Lower manual intervention
- Increased ROI

Summary

In this chapter, we have covered:

1. **EAI case study**: Here, we tried to develop a solution for a major FMCG industry. The various heterogeneous systems within the organization were integrated.

2. **EAI drawback**: We briefly discussed the drawback of designing solution based on EAI.

6
Goals We Can Achieve with SOA

SOA is mainly a mindset, an enterprise strategy whose natural implementation is represented by web services. In the early years, when the WS-approach began to emerge, it suffered from difficulties due to many factors such as complex adoption process and poor standardization. Now, the time has matured for using this technology with little effort while getting great advantages, both immediate and as an investment for our future works. In this chapter, we will go through the advantages of loose coupling, which is a key concept for an effective modular and extensible system. Then, we will show how SOA makes re-using easier with respect to traditional approaches. Designing pluggable services also favors the integration of processes, and guarantees a high degree of flexibility over time and technology changes. Finally, we will see how all these advantages contribute to raise the ROI.

Loose Coupling

The concept of "coupling" in software development comes into play at many levels. A common example is represented by the interface-implementation pattern, where the interface (also referred to as "contract") aims to decouple itself from the specific implementation(s). It can be generally defined as a measure of the dependencies among components. The more tightly one component is dependent on another, the more it is difficult to modify it without having to consider the impact of the modification on the rest of the system.

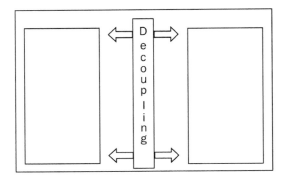

Keeping the overall measure of coupling low is therefore a good practice, maybe one of the more important indicators of a well-designed architecture. A loose-coupled system is easier to maintain, prone to evolving, and integrates better with other applications. In a word, it's the key-point of a successful architecture.

As we had mentioned earlier, loose coupling in general, can be applied in several ways in the programming field. One of the first examples of this pattern is the very basic concept of "interface" that every object-oriented language provides. Defining and using the interface in place of a concrete class (the implementation) is the first step towards loose coupling. This way, we obtain an independence from the concrete implementations of the interface. Hence, changing an implementation means no impact over the existing code wherever the interface is used.

Another example of loose coupling is the "Dependency Injection" mechanism provided by an **Inversion of Control (IoC)** container, such as Spring framework or PicoContainer. In this case, the container configuration, usually expressed by an XML file, allows us to "wrap" the various components together in a loose manner. Not only are we free to switch from one component implementation to another, but can also add or remove some orthogonal mechanisms (aspects) such as security or interceptors, just to make some examples. All this can be done by changing the configuration, without any modification of our code.

In the context of web services, though, the levels of loose coupling we can obtain extend this reach far beyond. Among these decoupling goals we can find:

- **Platform independence**: Thanks to the XML-based communication, we get a language-neutral approach. Therefore, the server and client platforms are completely independent (for example Java and .NET).

- **WSDL language-neutral aspect and automatic code generation**: Starting the design of a web service from its WSDL (contract-first approach) is a good practice since it allows us to have a language-neutral service definition. Furthermore, the code is automatically generated into the specific language. An example of automatic code generation from WSDL is shown in the following figure:

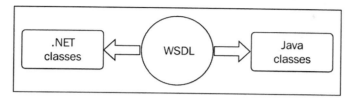

- **Document style**: The independence from the platform can also be obtained with CORBA or other RPC forms. Every RPC approach, however, means a heavy impact over the existing code, when it comes to changing the signature of a business method in the back-end. This is not a good practice, as back-end methods should not be exposed. Document style instead means easier maintenance and flexibility, since it involves thinking in terms of messages, rather than distributed-objects. Hiding business methods through document style is illustrated in the following figure:

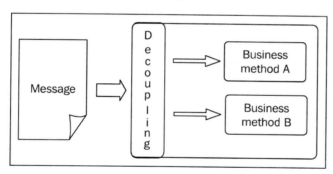

- **Flexibility and Fault-tolerance**: A change in the structure of an exchanged object's class is generally a critical operation when it comes to distributed applications. The overall impact is quite significant since the "actors" involved in the communication must be updated with the latest class version. This is not the case with web services. Thanks to the fact that objects are serialized and deserialized to and from an XML stream, most structural changes can be introduced with zero-impact. Let's take for instance the sample code (Listing 30 — SOAP Document wrapped web service) shown in Chapter 2 in the "Document/literal wrapped" section and add a new attribute, with correspondent getter/setter methods, in the class Outcome at server side:

```
public class Outcome {
    private String retCode;
    private String retMessage;
    private String other;

    . . .
}
```

The server module can now assign a value to the new attribute and the clients that update to the new Outcome class can receive that value. But what about the clients who do not update? Well, they will continue to work in the same way. They will obviously not be receiving the new value, but the deserialization process will not break. On the other side, we can remove an attribute (for example, retMessage) in the server module, and have a non-updated client receive a null value in this field, though still working.

- **Asynchronous communication**: Another important web service feature consists of being able to call a service in an asynchronous mode. This adds another level of loose coupling, since the caller module gains independence from the immediate availability of the called component, which for instance, may not be under our control.

It should be noted that there may be cases where tight coupling is better. In fact, low coupling has a price in terms of performance loss due to the introduction of interfaces. Furthermore, tight coupling allows strong type-safe checking at design time, which translates into robustness while loose coupling can only be checked at run time. Generally, the advantages of loose coupling in terms of modularity, flexibility, and scalability are considered to largely overcome its disadvantages.

Reusability

Programming by components and libraries is functional to layering software development and thus to re-using parts with a modular approach. The developer takes already developed libraries (from within the company's repository or third-party) and builds upon them.

In the same way, the web services approach is functional to layering business process composition, since it allows the WS-developer to re-use already running developed services. By re-using components, the developer uses libraries and the compiled code *should* run as desired. Now, by re-using services, what is exploited is running code. The re-used service, in fact, is presumably already serving other clients or other "consumer" modules. Remember that one service may call another service, acting as a client in that specific communication process.

The level of re-use of web services is one of the most significant indicators of a successful SOA initiative. In other words, re-use provides high business value. In fact, the higher the number of processes that re-use a service, lower the cost of that service, and the easier it is to maintain and to test the code. High reusability is a clear indicator of how good the service originally designed was. It is a sign of the farsightedness of the analyst and designer teams. The service should be as independent as possible from a specific application requirement, possibly throughout, making extensive use of parameterization, or by decomposing it into more fine-grained services. The goal is to make the service "survive" the scope of one or few applications, and become generic enough to serve a wide range of applications or business processes with a modular approach. Indeed, this result is generally obtained as an effect of consistent investments into the quality of development process and standardization aspects, where great effort can be spent in the phase of designing new services.

A high number of services should not be regarded as a good indicator of SOA success, but quite the opposite. It is the ratio between the number of business processes built upon the services, and the number of used services that gives an index of Reusability:

$$\text{Reusability index} = \frac{\text{Total number of Business Processes using Services}}{\text{Total number of Services}}$$

In the mid-to-long run, designing business processes or solutions can therefore become a matter of assembling services rather than creating new ones.

Seamless Integration

SOA is above all an integration-oriented design philosophy. It is a kind of approach that has been around since the beginning of the programming era. Indeed a number of legacy business functions, originally developed in COBOL or RPG, have been written following this paradigm. Many such pieces of code have survived most technology evolutions and are still running and often considered the most reliable and stable part in some systems. Being developed as shareable independent units, they can be seamlessly wrapped into web services today, and integrated in a SOA environment, and then survive again.

This teaches us an important lesson that when designing an application that is not intended to expose services, creating business functions with **software as a service (SaaS)** methodology is a winning practice. Thinking modular and shareable is the best insurance for our code, our work, and our design.

Integration may then happen at various levels. It can become a company's internal need, where new applications can be built exploiting already developed services. However, another interesting option is making a service available to others, thus exposing it externally. This paves the way for a new IT frontier.

The Internet is adding a new value to its nature as a repository of contents, explored by users through the browser. It is also becoming a container of business services that can be used by applications or accessed, joined and assembled to create new business processes. Manufacturers, suppliers, and customers (just to make an example) are becoming aware of the huge potential to be realized from adopting a service-oriented approach. This goes far beyond the **Electronic Data Interchange (EDI)** standardization introduced years ago to allow the **business-to-business (B2B)** data exchange. Now, the goals are the pluggability of services, and the overcoming of the B2B boundaries down to the consumer side that is **business-to-consumer (B2C)**.

Return on Investment (ROI)

From what we have discussed so far, it should be clear enough how SOA can lead to a better ROI. Indeed, these chapters are very interlaced one to the other.

Loose coupling, in fact, means easier maintainability, and hence a saving in the maintenance phase. But it also helps re-use, which translates into less work to be done while developing new business processes. Seamless integration, on the other hand, means reduced effort when it comes to putting together heterogeneous subsystems that need to interact.

- **Loose coupling**: Minimize maintainability effort
- **Reuse**: Exploit already developed services
- **Seamless Integration**: Reduce integration work

As you can see all these aspects are inherent to saving, and this could by itself be enough motivation to favor SOA adoption.

Saving, however, is not the only goal that SOA can lead to. It paves the way for new business opportunities since companies can react quickly and effectively to their customer's needs. Furthermore, the new development model, based on composition and the assembling of already available services, will disclose huge potentials for the business process designers.

Here is an analogy to help illustrate these potentials. Consider an exposed service analogous to an **Application Programming Interface (API)** of an operating system or a language. A set of API, possibly created by different third-parties, can be exploited by a developer to build a complex application or a specialized library. Similarly, a set of services from various sources can be used by a SOA designer to create a business process application or specifically, more complex libraries of services. This structured assembling process will not only boost the development by a significant factor, but will also allow rapid adaptation against the changes and evolution of the requirements.

Summary

In this chapter, we explored in detail the advantages that the SOA approach can lead to. Thanks to loose coupling, we can design at a higher level of abstraction, focusing on business concepts and actions, reducing the dependencies from the specific service implementation. Re-using can leverage the already developed services and therefore limit the development process to the creation of new services and assembling the existing ones. These factors are, on the other hand, key elements for a seamless integration within a flexible and adaptive information system. In the end, we learned that designing by services can help to build a solid infrastructure upon which we can plug our future projects. Nevertheless, we can also benefit from immediate advantages, since breaking the business processes down to their modular services allows for a better management, and opens the way to cooperation not only within the company, but also on behalf of third-party subjects.

Index

[PACKT] PUBLISHING Thank you for buying
Service Oriented Architecture
with Java

Packt Open Source Project Royalties

When we sell a book written on an Open Source project, we pay a royalty directly to that project. Therefore by purchasing Service Oriented Architecture with Java, Packt will have given some of the money received to the Apache Web Service and Apache SOAP project.

In the long term, we see ourselves and you—customers and readers of our books—as part of the Open Source ecosystem, providing sustainable revenue for the projects we publish on. Our aim at Packt is to establish publishing royalties as an essential part of the service and support a business model that sustains Open Source.

If you're working with an Open Source project that you would like us to publish on, and subsequently pay royalties to, please get in touch with us.

Writing for Packt

We welcome all inquiries from people who are interested in authoring. Book proposals should be sent to authors@packtpub.com. If your book idea is still at an early stage and you would like to discuss it first before writing a formal book proposal, contact us; one of our commissioning editors will get in touch with you.

We're not just looking for published authors; if you have strong technical skills but no writing experience, our experienced editors can help you develop a writing career, or simply get some additional reward for your expertise.

About Packt Publishing

Packt, pronounced 'packed', published its first book "Mastering phpMyAdmin for Effective MySQL Management" in April 2004 and subsequently continued to specialize in publishing highly focused books on specific technologies and solutions.

Our books and publications share the experiences of your fellow IT professionals in adapting and customizing today's systems, applications, and frameworks. Our solution-based books give you the knowledge and power to customize the software and technologies you're using to get the job done. Packt books are more specific and less general than the IT books you have seen in the past. Our unique business model allows us to bring you more focused information, giving you more of what you need to know, and less of what you don't.

Packt is a modern, yet unique publishing company, which focuses on producing quality, cutting-edge books for communities of developers, administrators, and newbies alike. For more information, please visit our website: www.PacktPub.com.

PACKT
PUBLISHING

Java EE 5 Development using
GlassFish
Application Server

The complete guide to installing and configuring the GlassFish
Application Server and developing Java EE 5 applications to be
deployed to this server

David R. Heffelfinger

PACKT

Java EE 5 Development using GlassFish Application Server

ISBN: 978-1-847192-60-8   Paperback: 400 pages

The complete guide to installing and configuring
the GlassFish Application Server and developing
Java EE 5 applications to be deployed to this server

1. Concise guide covering all major aspects of Java
   EE 5 development

2. Uses the enterprise open-source GlassFish
   application server

3. Explains GlassFish installation and
   configuration

4. Covers all major Java EE 5 APIs

BPEL Cookbook

Best Practices for SOA-based integration and composite
applications development

Ten practical real-world case studies combining business
process management and web services orchestration

Editors Harish Gaur   Markus Zirn

PACKT

BPEL Cookbook: Best Practices for SOA-based integration and composite applications development

ISBN: 1-904811-33-7   Paperback: 188 pages

Ten practical real-world case studies combining
business process management and web services
orchestration

1. Real-world BPEL recipes for SOA integration
   and Composite Application development

2. Combining business process management and
   web services orchestration

3. Techniques and best practices with
   downloadable code samples from ten real-
   world case studies

Please visit **www.PacktPub.com** for information on our titles

LaVergne, TN USA
15 September 2009
157847LV00003B/11/P